THE REPUBLIC OF SOUTH AFRICA
AND THE HIGH COMMISSION
TERRITORIES

The Republic of South Africa and the High Commission Territories

by

LORD HAILEY, O.M.

LONDON
OXFORD UNIVERSITY PRESS
NEW YORK   CAPE TOWN
1963

Oxford University Press, Amen House, London E.C.4

GLASGOW   NEW YORK   TORONTO   MELBOURNE   WELLINGTON
BOMBAY   CALCUTTA   MADRAS   KARACHI   LAHORE   DACCA
CAPE TOWN   SALISBURY   NAIROBI   IBADAN   ACCRA
KUALA LUMPUR   HONG KONG

Printed in Great Britain

by the Pitman Press, Bath

CONTENTS

CONTENTS

ACKNOWLEDGEMENTS

IN 1960 I began to collect material in order to bring up to date the study of the High Commission Territories which was published in 1953 as the fifth Part in the series *Native Administration in British African Territories*. But it became obvious that the relations of the three High Commission Territories as a whole with the Union of South Africa would, as the result of pending constitutional changes, soon provide greater public interest than the separate stories of their economic and political progress. I therefore diverted my efforts to the present booklet, which also made it possible to give a fuller treatment to past and present aspects of these relations than my original design had contemplated.

But I could not myself have completed the booklet had it not been fortunate enough to receive in its later stages the advice and assistance of Mr. C. E. Carrington and of his intimate knowledge of colonial affairs. I am greatly indebted to him for the help so kindly given to me.

I wish also to acknowledge the assistance rendered by Miss Katharine Duff and Miss Hermia Oliver in revising the proofs of the booklet and its preparation for publication.

August 1963   HAILEY

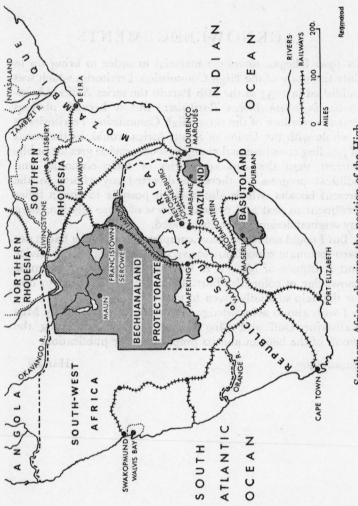

Southern Africa, showing the position of the High Commission Territories

INTRODUCTION

IT has been convenient to retain as the title of this work the term High Commission Territories, in order to denote the three British dependencies Bechuanaland, Basutoland, and Swaziland. In the Republic of South Africa the term 'Protectorates' is that normally employed in both parliamentary and journalistic usage; it is also frequently used in the British Parliament, though it is incorrect in so far as Basutoland has the full status of a British territory. These three dependencies, as will be shown in the following pages, were brought under the control of the High Commissioner in South Africa by virtue of the original enactments which established British jurisdiction over them.

The office of High Commissioner was in the first instance attached to that of the Governor of Cape Colony, and after 1909 to that of the Governor-General of South Africa. When, however, a constitutional practice was adopted in 1931, as the result of which the Governor-General was appointed on the advice of Ministers in the Union of South Africa, 'to represent the King's Grace and not the British Government', the office of High Commissioner was separated from that of the Governor-General. The High Commissioner to the Union thereafter occupied a position similar to that of the High Commissioners to other Dominions as the representatives of His Majesty's Government in the United Kingdom. In addition to the normal functions of that position, however, he remained responsible for the administration of Basutoland, the Bechuanaland Protectorate, and Swaziland, and in the legislation applicable to them he was expressly so designated. When in 1961 the Union became the Republic of South Africa and the High Commissioner became the British Ambassador to the Republic, he continued to be responsible for the administration of the three Territories.

There is no evidence that the exercise of dual functions

caused any special difficulty in the case of the Governors of
Cape Colony or the Governors-General who for a considerable period held also the office of High Commissioner.
Lord Selborne, for example, might well have felt some such
difficulty when as Governor of Cape Colony and High
Commissioner he took an active part in the discussions which
preceded the assembly of the National Convention of 1908
and the drafting of the Act of Union of 1909. His position as
Governor did not deter him from insisting as High Commissioner on the necessity for safeguarding the rights of the
Native peoples of the three Territories in the event of their
transfer to the Union.[1] Something of the same attitude was
exhibited by Lord Athlone as Governor-General and High
Commissioner in 1926, when dealing with General Hertzog's
proposal for the transfer of Swaziland to the administration
of the Union.[2] One inevitably recalls here the lesson conveyed
in Lord Radcliffe's reminder[3] that, though we are apt to take
great pride in the character of our British institutions, the real
significance lies in the character of those who have been called
upon to discharge the functions which those institutions have
involved.

The procedure now introduced, under which the Ambassador to the Republic will retain the post of High Commissioner,
has led to an active discussion of the advisability of arranging
for an effective separation of the two offices. This is not, it
may be noted, the first time that some attention has been given
to certain aspects of this question. As will subsequently be
shown, there was a somewhat prolonged period during which
the British Government appeared to show little interest in the
political or economic development of the three Territories. It
was not, indeed, until attention was directed to their situation
by the publication of the Reports made by Sir A. Pim in 1932
and the following years, that any serious steps were taken by
the British Government to aid in the process of their development.[4] The realization of the need for such aid provoked at

[1] See p. 29 ff.   [2] See p. 61–62.
[3] *The Problems of Power*, Reith Lectures, 1951.   [4] See p. 70 ff.

the time a discussion in official circles as to the advisability of appointing an officer of superior status who could give his undivided attention to their administration, and who could personally supervise schemes made for their social and economic advancement. No steps were, however, taken in this direction at the time; it was deemed sufficient to take in 1935 measures for the introduction of a system under which the administrative cadre in the Territories, hitherto recruited locally, would henceforward be recruited from the same sources and employed under the same conditions as the United Colonial Service.[5]

When the Union Government left the Commonwealth in 1961, there arose a wider and, to all appearance, a more profound interest in a change of the system under which the Ambassador would for the future carry out the functions of the High Commissioner. During the debates in Parliament on the passage of the South Africa Bill of 1962, the question appeared to be one of special concern, and there were speakers in both Houses who considered it essential that the Administrations of the three Territories should have at their head a Governor who would reside in one or other of the Territories, not in any part of the Republic. Up to date the Government has not announced a final decision on this point, though it appeared in the course of the debate that the Prime Minister had expressed some preference for retention of the practice under which the Ambassador would remain responsible for the discharge of the functions of the High Commissioner in respect of the Territories. Meanwhile, it has been stated that the Resident Commissioners in Swaziland and Bechuanaland will be made directly responsible to the Colonial Secretary for the government of their territories, and will be described as Her Majesty's Commissioners for their Territories. A similar arrangement is being considered for Basutoland.[6]

---

[5] See R. Furse, *Aucuparius: the Recollections of a Recruiting Officer* (Oxford University Press, 1962), pp. 246–52.

[6] *Hansard*, House of Commons, 26 February 1962 Cols. 1987, 1032–4, 1061–5; 29 March 1962, Cols. 1643–8. *Hansard*, House of Lords, 12 April 1962, Cols. 587–95, 597, 606, 638; 30 May 1963, Col. 953; 20 June 1963, Col. 1485.

It is also significant that effect has been given to a measure which has more than once come under discussion in the past, namely, the transfer of the charge of the Territories from the Commonwealth Relations Office to the Colonial Office. That is a step which might with advantage have been taken some years ago, both on general grounds and because the Colonial Office has on its establishment a number of technical advisers whose services might have been available to the Administrations of the Territories in carrying out schemes for the amelioration of their social and economic conditions.

I

THE TERRITORIES BEFORE 1909

BECHUANALAND, Swaziland, and Basutoland are widely separated from each other in point of geography. They have no close affinity in their ethnic composition. They became dependencies of Great Britain at different times and in different circumstances. But they have had a common concern in respect of their relation to the Union of South Africa as it existed from 1909 to 1961. That element of common concern goes far back into their history, for it is true to say that each of the Territories has owed its status as a British dependency either directly or indirectly to incidents arising from its contact with one or another of the States which in 1909 became part of the Union.

Their story can be shortly told. The declaration of a Protectorate in Bechuanaland in 1885 had for its avowed objective the protection of certain of the Bechuana tribes from the incursion of Boer citizens of the Transvaal Republic of the day or of the neighbouring mushroom republics of Goshen and Stellaland which were subsequently incorporated in that Republic. These incursions threatened to deprive the tribes of lands over which they had established their possession long before Boer trekkers had crossed the Vaal River. The Bechuana tribes which were most closely affected were those lying immediately to the south of the Molopo River. They had more than once sought some measure of protection from the Cape Government, and they had very valid reasons for welcoming the declaration of the Protectorate over Bechuanaland. A number of the important tribes lying to the north of the Molopo, as, for instance, the Ngwaketse, the Kwena, and the Ngwato, had been subjected to experiences which had made them apprehensive of future trouble from the Transvaalers, and some of them had indeed joined the tribes lying south of the Molopo (as for instance in 1870, 1874, and 1876) in seeking some measure of protection from the Cape Government. But the actual declaration of the Protectorate by Great Britain seems to have come as a surprise to some of them, and it was indeed for a time viewed by certain of them with suspicion.[1] Intimation of the declaration of the Protectorate does not seem to have been communicated until a later period to the tribes lying still farther to the north and to the north-west, as for example the Tswana or the Kalaka. These tribes had had some experience of Matabele depredations, but had little or no experience of the actual incursion of Boers from the Transvaal or from the two republics of Goshen and Stellaland.

What then, it may be asked, were the grounds for proclaiming a formal measure of protection over so extensive an area as Bechuanaland? It is true that much of it was then, as now, semi-desert and very sparsely inhabited. But the area covered by the declaration of the Protectorate was no less than 267,000 square miles, or considerably larger than that of France. The explanation is to be found in a combination of circumstances which for a time made the future of Bechuanaland an issue of some importance in the domestic politics of Great Britain.

It was a characteristic feature of British politics at this period that the issues on which the differences of the two major political parties were hammered out seemed to lie in the field of external affairs, rather than in those social or economic developments affecting the standards of life of the population which form the most engrossing topics of present-day politics. In the late seventies of the last century the problem of Irish Home Rule was already beginning to divide the allegiance of the Liberal Party, but there was also a marked measure of concern due to the news of the troubles arising in South Africa from the efforts made by the Transvaal to re-assert its independence of British sovereignty. Interest in this direction came to a head when British troops suffered a serious reverse at Majuba Hill in February 1881, and this was followed by the concession

---

[1] A. Sillery, *The Bechuanaland Protectorate* (O.U.P., Cape Town, 1952), pp. 29, 33, 60.

of self-rule to the Transvaal in the Pretoria Convention of
July of that year. The Government of Cape Colony, which at
the time was much troubled by local divisions and was unable
itself to face any onerous responsibility arising in the field of
external relations, had for some time been appealing to the
Imperial Government for its help in curbing the trespass by
'freebooters' from the Transvaal and from the republics of
Goshen and Stellaland into the tribal areas lying to the west
of its border. The Cape complained that these movements,
besides being a breach of Conventions made with the Transvaal, moreover jeopardized freedom of movement on the
important highway to the north (the so-called Missionaries'
Road) which lay just beyond the Transvaal border. The
protests of the Cape had strong support from humanitarian
interests in Great Britain and also from merchants and
Chambers of Commerce. Here, however, the strong 'radical'
element in the British Cabinet, traditionally opposed to any
extension of territorial responsibilities, succeeded in defeating
for the time being any suggestion of open interference with this
aspect of Transvaal activity. It is indeed doubtful whether the
instances of the Cape Government or the protests of humanitarian and commercial interests in Great Britain would have
succeeded in securing the formal declaration of a Protectorate
over the tribal area through which the road to the north ran,
to say nothing of the extensive area lying to the west and to the
north of Bechuanaland, if it had not been for a complication
which now arose in the field of international politics.

France, whose hostility had been aroused by evidence of the
growing hold acquired by Great Britain in Egypt, had established an *entente* with Germany which was directed towards
the curtailment of any further expansion of the British sphere
of interest in Africa. The British Foreign Office had some
reason to suspect a plot on the part of Germany to effect, with
the connivance of the Transvaal, an extension of its own sphere
of influence which would effectively bar British access to the
Sudan and Egypt. Advancing from the base already established in Angra Pequena in 1883, Germany proclaimed in

1884 a protectorate over Damara-Namaqualand, while there
was evidence that President Kruger was seeking to secure the
construction of a railroad linking up Pretoria with Angra
Pequena on the west and St. Lucia Bay on the east.[2] The
Cape Government, now seriously concerned, asked that the
whole area from the Transvaal border to Damaraland should
be brought under Imperial protection. In Great Britain the
Liberal Government, which was nearing the end of its term
of office, could no longer stand aside in face of the prospect
which now lay before it. It had maintained that in any formal
extension of the British sphere of influence to which it had con-
sented, its motive had always been defensive, not expansionist.
There was accordingly little need for critics to cavil at its
claim that it was acting in defence of British interests when it
now dispatched a military mission under Sir Charles Warren
to re-establish order in the area lying immediately beyond the
western border of the Transvaal. It is, however, not without
significance that in the Order in Council of 27 January 1885,
declaring a Protectorate over Bechuanaland, the area over
which protection was extended was described only in terms
of degrees of latitude and longitude, and it is also significant
that the initial communication made to Sir Charles Warren,
who was now charged as Special Commissioner to give effect
to the terms of the Order, instructed him to inform the tribes
that steps had been taken in London 'to warn Germany that
Bechuanaland and the Kalahari are now under British protection'.[3] It was in effect the British answer to the suspected
German-Transvaal conspiracy to establish a hegemony over
South Africa.

Within the government departments which had the responsibility of dealing with the practical implementation of issues
arising in the field of foreign policy, there had for long been a
division of opinion as to the method by which an extension of
Imperial responsibility could best be carried out, given that

[2] *Cambridge History of the British Empire* (1959), Vol. III, p. 139; E. A.
Walker, *A History of Southern Africa* (Longmans, 1957), pp. 400–3.
[3] Sillery, op. cit., pp. 53–59.

such an extension was either desirable or unavoidable. Was it to be by the direct use of Imperial agency, or was it, so to speak, to be carried out by proxy: that is to say, by extending the sphere of responsibility of an existing dependency, or by the creation of a chartered organization, or by some similar device for avoiding Imperial expenditure, military or civil? This was an issue in which the public took its own share of interest; the humanitarian or missionary interest and that of the major commercial concerns usually showed itself to be on the side of direct Imperial action. The issue arising from the creation of a Protectorate over Bechuanaland found highly interested advocates on both sides. It is unnecessary to discuss here the form of the arguments used; it is sufficient to say that in official discussions leading up to the decision to declare a Protectorate, it had been agreed between the Imperial Government and that of Cape Colony that (in the terms used at the time) 'Bechuanaland should go to the Cape'; but the High Commissioner and the Cape Ministers differed regarding the conditions on which incorporation into Cape Colony should take place. As a result, the Order in Council of January 1885 was followed by a Proclamation of 30 September of the same year, which declared as 'British territory' only the southern portion of the proclaimed area, which was now more closely defined as 'the area which lay south of the Molopo River and the Ramathlabana Spruit'. The area north of the Molopo River up to latitude 22 degrees was shown as 'remaining under Her Majesty's protection'. A further proclamation of 6 October of the same year appointed the Governor of Cape Colony to administer as a 'Crown Colony' the southern portion, henceforth to be known as British Bechuanaland. Some ten years afterwards, this area, amounting to 43,000 square miles, was formally incorporated in Cape Colony by an Order of October 1895. This had, among other things, the effect of bringing the important centre of Mafeking, as also the lesser centres of Vryburg and Kuruman, within the boundaries of Cape Colony. It does not seem that any of the Bechuana Chiefs in the area thus annexed were consulted before its

2

declaration as British territory, nor does it appear that its subsequent transfer to Cape Colony met with any comment from them. This is the more noticeable because the measure actually divided into two parts the area occupied by the Rolong tribe.[4] It may today be a matter of legitimate regret that the course of events has now brought the people of this area under the authority of the Government of the Republic of South Africa, whose concept of race relations differs so widely from that of the people of Great Britain. But it is not a result which could by any exercise of foresight have been anticipated in 1895.

It is thus clear that the relations of Bechuanaland with the residents of the Transvaal had been only in part responsible for the inclusion of the Bechuanaland Protectorate among British dependencies. Swaziland, however, stands in a very different category, for after a period of actual administration by the Transvaal it was treated as having passed under British jurisdiction, in company with the Transvaal itself. The Swazi could not at that period claim the same measure of independence as the Bechuana tribes had enjoyed before the declaration of the Protectorate in 1885; but they had on the other hand maintained a considerable measure of unitary control in regard to purely indigenous affairs. The Nkosi-Dlamini clan of the Nguni tribe had during the sixteenth century acquired definite ascendancy not only over the Nguni inhabitants of the area which was to become recognized as Swaziland, but also over most of the Sotho tribes included in it. In the middle of the nineteenth century, Mswati, the Paramount Chief of the Dlamini, aided by the use of a development of the age-group system, secured a position which was equivalent to sovereignty over the whole area. It was in his reign that Europeans first came in some numbers into the Swazi country. There is no record of organized incursion, but Europeans arrived as individuals both from the Transvaal and from Natal. The Swazi had suffered much from the attacks of bands of Zulu, the remnants of groups which had originally been set adrift in

[4] Sillery, op. cit., pp. 77, 78, 174.

the chaos caused by the reign of terror established by the Zulu chief Shaka, and both the Boers of the Transvaal and the British of Natal came to be regarded by Mswati as possible allies against the Zulu. The Transvaal Government was more-over anxious to maintain friendly relations with the Swazi, for it was at the time seeking to gain access to the sea, and it seemed that the Swazi country might provide a convenient route to Kosi Bay, the projected harbour in Tongaland. But there were also other grounds for the interest of the Transvaal burghers, for they valued highly the grazing rights available to them beyond the actual Transvaal border.[5] Between 1875 and 1881 the burghers had in various ways shown a practical interest in the maintenance of order within Swaziland, and in 1875 a commando had been sent to aid in suppressing the con-flict which was beginning to arise over the disputed succession to the position of Paramount Chief. In doing so, the commando had supported the claims made by one of the junior aspirants, Mbandzeni, who was eventually proclaimed as Paramount. It was asserted at the time that an agreement had been made by his supporters which would ensure the acquisition by the Transvaal Government of a definite measure of control over Swazi affairs; but it does not seem that this agreement was actually ratified by the Volksraad. On the other hand, the Government of Natal was anxious to avoid the acquisition by the Transvaal of any such hold over Swaziland as might make Boer progress to the sea more feasible and thus open up a port for the sole use of the Transvaal. When, therefore, the Conven-tion of Pretoria was under negotiation with the Transvaal in 1881, Natal secured the inclusion of a provision that formally guaranteed the independence of Swaziland, and this provision was duly repeated in the London Convention of 1884.

But it soon became less necessary for the Transvaal to contend for the overt recognition of political authority over Swaziland. At an earlier stage Mswati had already begun to make considerable concessions of land rights to Europeans coming from the Transvaal. He had gone further, and in 1855

[5] *Annual Report, Swaziland, 1959*, p. 117.

had sold to the Transvaal an area (mainly occupied by Sotho tribesmen) which embraced most of the present Lydenburg district. His successor Mbandzeni carried the same process to extremes. He conceded to Europeans a great number of mining rights and monopolies of all kinds, including trading rights, and even rights to collect customs and revenue. These concessions were subsequently described as having been 'of the most amazing scope, variety, and intricacy'. It is, however, proper to add that though some of these were granted for long periods, there was nearly always a limit of time imposed, nor did the Swazi regard land concessions as diminishing their own right to the concurrent use of the land, however difficult the exercise of such a right might prove in practice. The concessions of land rights were held mainly by Transvaal Boers; those of other kinds were held by Europeans from Natal as well as from the Transvaal; a number were also held by mining companies operating from Europe. There was inevitably a confusion of title between the concessionaires, and as a result the Natal Government was drawn into efforts to arbitrate in these disputes, though neither that Government nor that of the Transvaal possessed the judicial or administrative capacity to execute the awards of the arbitrators. In the effort to secure these powers the Transvaal Government sought to obtain from the British a modification of the provision in the Conventions of 1881 and 1884 which had formally guaranteed the independence of Swaziland. The British Government, which seemed at first inclined to accept this proposal, was faced by the protests of British Chambers of Commerce and the owners of mining concessions, and for a short period an effort was made to meet the situation by a system of dual control over all issues in which persons other than Swazi were concerned. But the Convention of 1890, in which British and Transvaal Governments agreed to this device, expressly recognized the sovereignty of the Swazi nation in respect of all affairs in which Natives alone were concerned. As a result, a Civil Court appointed for the purpose dealt with a considerable number of the concessions, though it took what now seems to be an unduly limited view of its own powers and functions; in administrative matters the working of the 'Provisional Government Committee' was hampered by disputes between Boers and British residents, while the course of Native affairs was complicated by disputes regarding the succession to Mbandzeni, who died in 1889. In 1893 the growing strength of the Boer residents led to an attempt on their part to secure Swazi agreement to a proposal that full rights of administration over Swaziland should be secured to the South African Republic, though without actual incorporation of Swaziland into the Republic. On this, the Swazi Queen Regent and her Council dispatched a deputation to England to plead that the British should take Swaziland under their protection. At this stage the future of Swaziland became one of the current issues of British party politics; on the one hand, there remained an active fear of a German-Transvaal collaboration in promoting a railway to Kosi Bay; on the other hand, an apprehension that any assumption of British administration over Swaziland might involve the Imperial Exchequer in responsibilities which, if undertaken at all, should be met by Natal, not by the Imperial Treasury.[6] Eventually Great Britain concluded with the Transvaal Government a Convention (10 December 1894) which gave the Transvaal Republic 'all rights of protection, legislation, jurisdiction, and administration over Swaziland', subject only to the condition that it should not be incorporated in the Transvaal. In 1895 the Transvaal Government appointed a Resident Special Commissioner to administer the country, and he occupied that position until the outbreak of the Anglo-Boer War in 1899. He then formally handed over his authority to the Queen Regent as Paramount Chief.

At the end of the war the Queen Regent requested that Swaziland should be annexed by the British and incorporated in the 'Transvaal Colony'. But in the negotiations leading to the Peace of Vereeniging, it had been agreed that the Transvaal would before long be given 'representative institutions leading up to self-government', and the British Government

[6] *Cambridge History of the British Empire*, loc. cit., p. 176.

decided that it would be advisable to retain a separate position for Swaziland. It preferred therefore to regulate its status under the terms of the Foreign Jurisdiction Act of 1890.[7] Thus the British Government acquired for itself the fullest powers of legislation and jurisdiction in Swaziland,[8] but the country has not been annexed as British territory. It was in pursuance of these powers that Swaziland was for purpose of convenience handed over in the first instance to the administration of the British Governor of the Transvaal. His post terminated in 1906, with the grant of Responsible Government to the Transvaal, and the authority which had been conferred on him was then transferred to the High Commissioner for South Africa.

Though the history of the extension of British jurisdiction over Basutoland has followed a different pattern from that of Swaziland, it nevertheless contains the same characteristic record of relations with a component state of the Union of South Africa, though in this case it was the Orange Free State and not the Transvaal which was mainly concerned. The story of the measures by which Moshesh, the titular founder of the Basuto nation, began during the early part of the nineteenth century to weld into one people a number of tribes in the Caledon Valley, stands out as one of the epics of indigenous African history. But for our present purpose it will suffice to begin at the stage when, in the course of the Great Trek of 1836, parties of Boer farmers began to search for pasture land on the upper reaches of the Orange River. A few pre-Trek Boers had already made a temporary settlement there as early as 1825, when they had found the countryside untenanted owing to the devastation caused by Zulu raids. But when a party from the Great Trek arrived ten years afterwards it found the locality populated by Basuto tribesmen who had returned under shelter of the rule of Moshesh. Boer farmers, separating

[7] Swaziland Order in Council 25 June 1903. See *Native Administration in British African Territories* (H.M.S.O., 1954), Pt. V, pp. 44, 270.
[8] For powers derived from the Foreign Jurisdiction Act of 1890 see *An African Survey* (1957), p. 285 ff.

from the main body of the Great Trek, came in increasing numbers to settle along the Caledon River and in the angle between it and the Orange River. It was with Moshesh that they settled for such dues as they paid for occupation of the land, though it is said that in order to safeguard himself against any claims which they might make for its ownership, he refused to take from them the 'pego', the customary due paid to a ruling Chief as guardian of the land. In his own phrase, he had only 'lent them the cow to milk'.

It was, however, inevitable that friction should arise on this score. In theory (but only of course in theory) the Boers were still subjects of the Cape Government, and late in 1839 and again in 1842 Moshesh had to protest to the Lieutenant-Governor at the Cape against the arbitrary conduct of the White farmers. In the latter year, indeed, he went so far as to ask the terms on which the British Crown would be willing to 'recognize' the tribe of the Basuto. On the latter occasion he received a more helpful reply than on the former, and in 1845 Sir G. Napier made an agreement with him in which he referred to him as 'a friend and ally of Cape Colony', and described the boundaries of his territories as recognized by the Cape Government. These, the agreement said, comprised all the country between the Orange and Caledon Rivers from their sources and beyond the Caledon to a distance of 25 or 30 miles, save for a small tract known as Bethuli. But it remained one of the major causes of trouble with the Boers who were settling in the Free State that the actual boundary was not demarcated, while the area on the Caledon was attracting settlement not only by them, but also by an increasing number of Basuto tribesmen.

It would be out of place here to deal at any length with the intervention by Major Warden, the representative of the Governor of Cape Colony, into the relations of the Basuto and the Free State Boers. He laid down a boundary line between the Boers and the Basuto in the Orange-Caledon angle. To Moshesh, however, this seemed to deprive the Basuto of lands which Napier's Agreement had assigned to them, while in his endeavour to overcome the Basuto refusal to accept his boundary line Warden appears to have both misapprehended the attitude of Moshesh and underestimated the fighting strength of the tribesmen at his disposal. In an attempt to intimidate the Basuto he led against them a body of levies which included a number of Free State burghers, but he was driven back in a fight at the Viervoet Plateau. Even more significant was the repulse at the Berea of a considerable regular force led by General Cathcart, which had been brought up from the Cape in order to counteract the effect of the indignity inflicted on Warden's levies. Moshesh, as diplomatic as he was resolute, took the occasion to impress on Cathcart that he still desired to remain a friend of the Queen of England, and he deliberately allowed Cathcart to extricate his force without serious loss. But the essence of the trouble which had arisen still remained, and would have been beyond the capacity of either Warden or Cathcart to remove. The recognition in 1854 of the independence of the Orange Free State had removed even the pretence of control by the Governments of the Cape or Natal over the incursions of the Free State Boers. The Free State organization, still weak and inexperienced, was not only unable but unwilling to attempt any restraint over its own burghers. The Basuto, now in a fighting mood, were ready to avenge the wrongs done to them by the Boer occupation of the fertile Caledon lands to which they felt, not without some reason, that they had established a prior claim.

The position was now aggravated by the fact that Moshesh had himself never acknowledged the boundary originally laid down by Napier, and an appeal made by him to the Governor of Natal showed that the British themselves no longer regarded the line as authoritative. When therefore the President of the Free State categorically demanded in 1858 that the Basuto should accept and abide by the line, Moshesh flatly refused. The Free State levies then invaded Basutoland. They were driven back in confusion, and the Basuto in their turn set themselves to ravage the neighbouring Boer farms. It required

the mediation of Sir George Grey, now Governor of Cape
Colony, to bring hostilities to a temporary halt. A new complication arose when the arbitration in which he attempted
to meet the claims of the Free State Boers gave them a considerable area which the Basuto had occupied for some time
and from which Moshesh either would not or could not
remove them.

Sir George Grey's successor, Sir Philip Wodehouse, failed
equally as a mediator, and fighting flared up again in 1865.
But the position of the two parties was now different from that
of 1858. The Free State had gained in population and in
leadership, and had in addition received from the Transvaal
the assistance which had formerly been refused to it. Moshesh
was feeling his age and he no longer retained so strong a
personal hold over the Basuto Chiefs. He had, moreover, lost
the goodwill of the Governor when his unruly nephew,
Ramanella, had made a raid into Natal in pursuit of some
Boer freebooters. It would be unwelcome to dwell in detail on
the pitiable tale which now began to unfold itself. Moshesh,
driven to extremities, found himself constrained to subscribe
in April 1866 to an agreement, known as the Treaty of Thaba
Bosigo, which would have yielded to the Free State the greater
part of Upper and Central Basutoland. This emergency,
which might well have meant the end of independence for the
Basuto, proved in fact to open a way to their salvation. Sir
Philip Wodehouse, seeing the Free State preparing to incorporate practically the whole of Basutoland into its own territory, realized the possibility that the Free State Boers might
be encouraged to seek even further expansion, and thus to gain
access to a port on the coast. Moshesh, in his growing debility,
had handed over his powers to his elder son Letsie, but had
urged him to secure protection from the British, whatever
might be the cost to the Basuto. He himself wrote an appeal to
Sir Philip Wodehouse asking that 'we may in all concerns,
duties and privileges become the faithful and true subjects of
Her Majesty's Government'. Wodehouse now decided to take
a course which his repugnance to the expansion of British

jurisdiction had previously prevented, and early in 1866 he began to urge the Imperial Government to intervene between the Free State Boers and the Basuto. The position was in one respect critical. If Basutoland was to be broken up, this could not be done without sending a stream of broken and desperate men pouring into Natal and Cape Colony. The Free State itself was now practically bankrupt, and was seeking to carry on its attack on Basutoland by calling on volunteers, mainly from British territory, to be paid in captured cattle and farms in the conquered territory. The retirement of Great Britain south of the Orange in 1854 had been an error, for it had isolated Natal, while even in Great Britain there were those who had begun to hold that the position could only be retrieved by taking a firm line in regard to Basutoland, now the storm centre of a growing state of chaos. In December 1867 the Secretary of State, who had originally expressed the same objection as Sir Philip Wodehouse to the extension of British rule, now authorized the annexation of Basutoland to the Colony of Natal.[9]

In intimating that Basutoland should be annexed to Natal, the Secretary of State no doubt had in view the differences existing between the local Governments in Cape Town and Durban as the result of the recent incorporation of the Transkei and Griqualand, in which Cape Colony appeared to have gained the greater advantage. Cape Colony was moreover due to receive its status of Responsible Government, and might prove to that extent to be less amenable to administrative directions issued by the Imperial Government. The matter remained for some time in debate between the High Commissioner and the Imperial Government and meanwhile the Free State levies continued to press hard on the Basuto, in order to anticipate the inclusion of their lands in British territory. Sir Philip Wodehouse was finally driven to issue a Proclamation on 12 March 1868, which declared the Basuto to be 'for all intents and purposes British subjects', and that their territory 'shall be, and shall be taken to be British

[9] Walker, op. cit., pp. 318–26.

Territory'.[10] The boundary between Basutoland and the Free State was adjusted in the Second Treaty of Aliwal North in February 1869, by which the Free State gained a valuable strip of land to the west of the Caledon. In the following July the Secretary of State, yielding to the insistent remonstrances of the High Commissioner, decided against the incorporation of Basutoland in Natal, and for the time being it was described as a 'Crown Protectorate' which was to be administered by the High Commissioner. In 1871 it was annexed to Cape Colony by an Act of Annexation passed by its Legislature.[11] This was not perhaps the most appropriate solution, for Natal, which still retained much of the Shepstone tradition, might well have proved to be a more experienced authority in dealing with the Basuto Chiefs.

The local administrative officers in Cape Colony found that the Basuto had suffered very severely from the attacks of the Free State levies. 'Large numbers of the people had migrated in search of work elsewhere; the remainder were crushed and humbled; the people were so dispersed that all organization was lost.' It is clear, however, that material conditions quickly improved under a rule of law and order. On the other hand, the early attempt of the Administration to carry out the policy indicated by Sir Philip Wodehouse, which had relied on the use of the Chiefs as agencies of local rule, soon gave place to the use of the 'magisterial system' in force in the Cape, both for general reasons, and because the Chiefs proved to be in a constant state of insubordination to the Paramount Chief. The people, whose experience had left them with a legacy of grave apprehension for their future, devoted to the purchase of arms much of the proceeds from the sale of their livestock or from their earnings by service in the Vaal River Diamond Fields, which from about 1870 began to provide a market for their labour.[12] This process indeed went so far that the Basutoland of this period could afterwards be described as 'the powder magazine of South Africa'[13] Experience was to show

[10] See Cmd. 8707, 1952, p. 103.   [11] Act 12 of 1871.
[12] *An African Survey*, p. 1487.   [13] Walker, op. cit., p. 353.

that the tribesmen retained under their new administration much of the tradition of independence on which Moshesh had been able to rely, and when they had to face in 1880 and the following years the consequence of the policy of disarmament which had since 1878 been adopted by the Cape Government, they broke out in open resistance. The so-called Gun War which followed involved much desultory fighting, of which the Cape Government seemed to have been the first to tire. It had spent nearly £3,000,000 on the war, and had in truth little to show for it. In the early part of 1883, it approached the Imperial Government with a request to be relieved of the charge of Basutoland. The circumstances in which this proposal came before the Cabinet differed widely from those which had in 1867 created such reluctance to accept the proposal to assume jurisdiction over Basutoland; the Cabinet was now constrained to look at colonial questions under the influence of those wider aspects of Imperial policy which were in 1885 to lead to the declaration of the Protectorate over Bechuanaland.[14]

The Imperial Government had not consulted the Basuto Chiefs before handing over their country to the charge of the Cape Government in 1871. It now decided, however, to ask them whether they preferred to come under the charge of an Imperial agency, or to return to the position which they had occupied before they were taken under the protection of the Crown. It would not, it said, be willing to resume charge of an unwilling or divided people. In November 1883 the major Basuto Chiefs signified that they wished to become British subjects 'under the direct rule of the Queen'.[15] The Cape Parliament had passed in September 1883 a Basutoland Disannexation Act, and a Proclamation was issued in March 1884, which brought Basutoland again under the rule of the Imperial Government. It is significant, however, that the latter had stipulated that the Cape Government should guarantee a payment of £20,000 a year, in case the revenues of Basutoland should prove inadequate to meet the cost of the services involved.

[14] See p. 6 ff. above.   [15] *Native Administration*, Pt. V, pp. 47–56.

The formal declaration of a British Protectorate in Bechuana-land, of sovereignty in Basutoland, and of the right of jurisdiction in Swaziland brought to a close one chapter in the relation of these Territories with the four States which were afterwards to become component units of the Union of South Africa. That chapter had reflected an attitude towards these Territories which was inspired not so much by an ambition for the expansion of the four States concerned as by the more limited purpose of finding fresh lands for the occupation of their farmers. But it had led to incidents which were due sometimes to ignorance and at other times to open disregard for the rights established by African tribesmen. They had led in some cases to a deplorable sacrifice of life and to the breakdown of tribal institutions. This period was now to be followed by one in which the interest of the States concerned was no longer to be directed so strongly to the support of farming interests, while their political activity was to be increasingly diverted to the effort to find some means of adjusting the relations between the different European communities within their own borders. External policy was to be increasingly concerned with the endeavour to find some means of adjusting the effects of inter-state rivalries in regard to the adjustment of customs dues or the routes to be taken by railways and highways. In such matters the High Commission Territories were little concerned. They could rest secure under the protection of the Imperial Government. That Government seemed for its part to be content with having provided for them a guarantee for the maintenance of security from outside attack, while leaving other matters mainly to the charge of the Native Authorities who provided such measure of local rule as was consonant with Native custom. It is not unnatural to find therefore that, so far as any question of social or economic development was concerned, the period was for some years one of relative stagnation.

In the Anglo-Boer War which broke out in 1899, the High Commission Territories took no part, and had in fact little concern, other than in such adventitious addition to their revenue as was provided by the service of tribesmen as transport workers or (as in the case of Basutoland) by the sale of horses or pack animals. When the war seemed imminent, the Native Authorities were informed, on the instructions of the High Commissioner, that the conflict would be one between the White races only, in which therefore Africans must take no part. On 12 October 1899, the Boers cut the railway line south of Mafeking, and soon afterwards a Boer force built a small stone fort near the boundary of the Bechuanaland Protectorate. At one stage the administrative staff at Gaberones was evacuated, and for a time the railway was put out of action. The column commanded by Colonel Plumer which was designed to assist in the relief of Mafeking passed through the east of the Protectorate. But these incidents had little influence on the African life of the Territory.[16] The Swazi people similarly accepted the injunction of the High Commissioner to preserve neutrality, and the only incident involving the Swazi area seems to have been the burning of the office formerly occupied by the Boer Administrator at Bremersdorp. Under similar advice the Basuto held aloof from the combat, though the Paramount Chief Lerotholi was obliged to exert his influence in order to defeat the efforts made by Free State agents to persuade the tribesmen to break their neutrality. These efforts succeeded in fact in the case of one Chief, Joel, though he seems to have taken up arms mainly in order to secure some aid from the Free State in support of a family quarrel.

In the course of the long and complicated peace talks which preceded the Treaty of Vereeniging in 1902, the actual discussions seem to have been concerned as much with constitutional issues as with those arising directly out of the war. The delegates of the two Boer Republics at first stood out stubbornly for a declaration of their independence; failing to secure this, they put forward proposals for the establishment of a British Protectorate over the two States. The British representatives finally found it politic to concede that, as soon as circumstances permitted, 'representative institutions tending

[16] Sillery, op. cit., p. 89.

towards self-government' should be introduced. With a range of discussion that went so far beyond immediate military issues, it was not unnatural that reference should also be made to the possibility that 'two at least of the three dependent territories' should be incorporated within the boundaries of either the Transvaal or the Orange Free State. It was a proposal that must have seemed all the more natural since, as the Peace Treaty conceded, the two Republics were now to come under the sovereignty of the British Crown. But divergent outlooks were revealed when questions arose regarding the future treatment of their Native inhabitants. Lord Milner, it seems, had pressed for an assurance that they should be entitled to the benefit of the measure of enfranchisement extended to Natives in Cape Colony, and the Colonial Secretary had informed him that the enfranchisement of such Natives as were qualified by education would be among the list of conditions regulating the actual grant of the measure of self-government forecast in the Peace Treaty. Both parties were however anxious that if possible nothing should delay the conclusion of the Peace Treaty, and it was therefore settled that the matter should stand over until the introduction of some form of self-government in the two Republics. We are told that Lord Milner afterwards regretted bitterly this postponement, for the treatment accorded to Africans had been put forward as one of the reasons for the war. He was, however, constrained to accept it.[17]

But when the two Boer Republics received in 1906 and 1907 their constitution of Responsible Government, a decision on the question of the incorporation of the three Territories had again to be deferred. It had by now become obvious that the Transvaal Boers could not be persuaded to abate their opposition to the enfranchisement of Natives. A Native Affairs Commission appointed in Cape Colony in 1903 had paid

[17] Article 8 of the Treaty of Vereeniging. See also L. M. Thompson, *The Unification of South Africa, 1902–1910* (Clarendon Press, 1960), p. 401; M. Perham and L. Curtis, *The Protectorates of South Africa* (O.U.P., 1935); C. Dundas and H. Ashton, *Problem Territories of Southern Africa* (1952), p. 30; *Cambridge History of the British Empire*, Vol. III, p. 372.

particular attention to the working of the Native franchise in the Colony. At the time there were in the Cape Colony a total of 142,367 voters. Of these 85·2 per cent. were Whites, 10·1 per cent. Coloured, and 4·7 per cent. African. Among other points the Commission had shown that in certain of the constituencies the African vote had been strong enough to determine the issue of an election. This appears to have added force to the traditional objection of the Transvaaler to the grant of political rights to Africans. The readiness to grant the formal status of Responsible Government to the Transvaal and the Free State so soon after the conclusion of the war was an 'act of faith' which won for the Liberal Government of Great Britain the goodwill of some of the best of its former opponents in the two States, but it did not carry sufficient support among them to enable the British Government to provide that the grant of Responsible status should ensure the provision of African enfranchisement in their new constitution.

History is at the same time not clear as to the process by which the Liberal Government came to accept this conclusion. Early in December 1906 General Smuts arrived in England, bringing a joint Memorandum from General Botha and himself which embodied proposals for giving effect to that programme of 'reconciliation' between Boers and British to which they both attached so great an importance. They insisted on a demand for Responsible Government in place of the Representative Government for which provision had been made in the Lyttelton Constitution and to which the outgoing Conservative Government had been committed. But the Memorandum made no proposal for the grant of enfranchisement to Africans. Had Smuts then forgotten the prophecy he had made in his student days, that eventual competition for political power in Africa would 'create a race struggle such as the world had never seen' ?[18] Clearly he was so far absorbed in his immediate task as to feel that the inclusion of mention of a Native vote might stand in the way of an early settlement of the issue of Responsible Government.

[18] See W. K. Hancock, *Smuts: the Sanguine Years* (C.U.P., 1962), p. 30.

It is less easy to understand how the West Ridgeway Constitutional Commission, charged to study the alternative propositions of Representative and Responsible Government, should to all appearance have neglected to raise this issue. No report of the proceedings of the Commission has been published, but it is known that many whom the Commission had consulted, and in particular J. X. Merriman, had made a very impressive demand for the extension of the Cape Native franchise. But when the Letters Patent announcing the new Constitution were issued in December 1906 no provision was made for the introduction of the Native vote. It was at this stage that the administration of Swaziland was (as already shown) transferred to the High Commissioner at the Cape. And it was also at this stage that the British Government, no doubt realizing the inconsistency of attitude it had taken in regard to the question of the Native vote, now declared that 'pending any grant of representation to natives, no territory administered by the Governor or High Commissioner will be placed under the control of the new Responsible Government'.[19] To this extent, therefore, the two issues, namely, the extension of the Native franchise and the incorporation of the High Commission Territories, had now become interdependent.[20] Moreover, the statement now made by the British Government had consequences which could not easily have been foreseen at the time it was made. The progressive changes in the economy and social conditions of the two Northern States in particular seemed bound to diminish the importance which they attached in 1906 to the incorporation of the High Commission Territories, so that the question was in fact likely to become in time one mainly of convenience and expediency. But the fact that incorporation of the Territories should have been refused to the two Northern States on grounds which implied the condemnation of a policy so firmly followed by a large section of their Afrikaner community gave the issue a new significance. It created in the two former Republics a strong and (as subsequent events have shown) a persistent urge to demand

[19] Dundas and Ashton, op. cit., p. 30.   [20] Thompson, op. cit., p. 124.

3

transfer of the Territories from British control to that of the Union. In the narrative which follows, insistence on this demand seems to have become a symbol of the growing ascendancy of the Afrikaner element in Union politics. Not only so, but it was to become in time part of the case which leaders of the Afrikaner community could put forward for the creation in South Africa of a State entirely independent of any vestige of control by the British Parliament or people. But these were developments for a still distant future. Only a few years after the grant of Responsible Government to the two Republics the question of the status of the three Territories became an important issue in the discussions regarding the creation of the Union of South Africa.

II

DISCUSSIONS DURING THE NATIONAL CONVENTION

THE biographer of General Smuts has said that many South African patriots had hoped to find in the amalgamation of the four South African States a reply to the imperialist designs which appeared to them to characterize a large section of the British at the end of the Anglo-Boer War. But the practical consummation of this ideal might have been long delayed but for the general realization of the difficulties arising from the clash of economic interests in these countries. Their concern had previously been limited to agricultural if not indeed purely pastoral development, but was now to embrace a much wider range of interests. So far as these differences took a racial aspect, their root lay in circumstances not unlike those which had divided the Dutch and British inhabitants of the Cape in the early part of the nineteenth century, but they were now manifested in a complex of antagonisms on policies relating to tariffs, customs duties, labour migration, highway and railway communications, and the like. Lord Milner had in 1903 presided over a Customs Conference at Bloemfontein which had gone some way to remove the tariff wall between the four States, and he had hoped to find here the basis of some form of federation between them. But since that date the four States had drifted further apart, and at one time it even seemed likely that the Customs Union itself would be broken up. In a number of quarters, and in particular among the group of civil officers who had been recruited by Lord Milner to assist in reorganizing the services of the two Colonies of which he was Governor,[1] discussions were in active progress, though so far on an unofficial basis, in the attempt to devise

[1] Thompson, op. cit., p. 61 ff.

some measure of unification of the four States which would suffice to solve the concrete problems to which their mutual rivalries now tended to give an acute form. In January 1907, the matter was brought within the range of practical politics by the issue of a Memorandum by Lord Selborne, which owed much to the work of the above-mentioned group of civil officers. The position of the Memorandum as one of the great dynamic documents of British Imperial history is due to the fact that it did not limit itself to pressing the case for 'closer union' merely on the ground that this could provide the remedy for the rivalries which were obstructing the economic progress of South Africa, but because it held that unification was essential to create the independent self-governing unit which could alone provide an instrument for adjusting the relations between the different racial and communal units which were represented in the four South African States. For present purposes it is noteworthy that the Memorandum saw unification as including all Colonies and Protectorates under British South African administration.[2] In July 1907 the Cape Parliament accepted a motion to appoint delegates to a National Convention which would discuss the general question of unification. Other State legislatures shortly followed suit.

It would not seem that in the many preliminary discussions which preceded the assembly of the National Convention the question of the incorporation of the three High Commission Territories formed one of the more important topics. But that it was discussed in some detail in at least one important quarter is clear. It would also seem that among a considerable number of the delegates there was an implicit assumption that it was 'inevitable that in time the government of these areas must be entrusted to the people of South Africa'. The question, moreover, already had a significant if somewhat contentious history of its own, and it was doubtless with this history in

---

[2] Thompson, op. cit., p. 67 ff; R. H. Brand, *The Union of South Africa* (O.U.P., 1909), pp. 111–12; Walker, op. cit., p. 520 ff; Perham and Curtis, op. cit., pp. 14, 32; *The Selborne Memorandum on the Union of South Africa* (O.U.P., 1925).

his mind, and in particular the declaration made by the British Cabinet in 1906, that Lord Selborne wrote to Sir Henry de Villiers, the Chairman of the Convention, emphasizing that

the obligations of His Majesty's Government to the tribes inhabiting Basutoland and the Bechuanaland Protectorate are obligations of the greatest possible weight. These tribes surrendered themselves under the dominion of Queen Victoria of their own free will, and they have been loyal subjects . . . ever since. The history and connexion of Swaziland is different, but the obligations are different only in degree.

Sir Henry de Villiers, who had recently visited England, announced to the Convention that the Imperial Government wished to give the delegates a free hand in everything but the Native franchise and the Protectorates, for 'it regarded itself in a special sense as a guardian and trustee of the Natives of South Africa'. He indicated his own view that 'if the settlement of the franchise question was regarded as unsatisfactory, then the Protectorates would not be handed over'.[3]

In the course of the discussions which preceded the meeting of the Convention there had emerged two different schools of thought regarding proposals for unification. One school had hoped to find a solution in some type of federation. This was preferably to be loose in form, since the inhabitants of the Orange Free State and those of Natal both feared, each from their own point of view, that they might be swamped by the Cape or the Transvaal.[4] There were among the Cape delegates those who felt almost passionately that the Union should set its seal on the extension of the Cape Native franchise throughout South Africa, and hoped that it might be more possible to attain this under a system of federation than under one of 'Closer Union'. But the advocates of the principle of 'Closer Union' proved to be the more active, and their views were propagated in a wide series of Closer Union Societies. In this process the group of Lord Milner's subordinates referred to

---

[3] Dundas and Ashton, op. cit., p. 30; Perham and Curtis, op. cit., p. 12.
[4] Walker, op. cit., p. 530; Thompson, op. cit., p. 186 ff.

above also took a very prominent part. When the Convention assembled, the advocates of federation failed to press their case to a vote, and the possibility of achieving some type of Closer Union became the ruling topic. The advocates of federation did indeed carry their case to England, and when the draft Union Bill was under discussion in Parliament, pressed it with some vigour, though with little success, on the public notice. In doing so, their main objective had been the safeguarding of the Cape Native franchise. For our present purpose the difference which arose on this point is important, since it seems clear that if the resultant measure of unification had in fact taken the form of federation, the question of the incorporation of the Territories, when subsequently raised, would have tended to become an issue between the individual States primarily concerned with schemes for incorporation, and would not have formed matter for the judgement of the Government of the Union as a whole. Both the pressure behind the demand for incorporation and the arguments on which the decision was to be based might thus have taken a far narrower scope.

It is also of importance that, when the Convention met, there was manifest from the first a wide cleavage between the delegates as a whole, turning mainly on the difference of view between those from the South, who held to the concept of 'equal rights for all civilized men', and those from the North, who were by tradition disposed to deny any measure of enfranchisement to Africans. It was in effect the cleavage of principle on this point which became one of the decisive factors in influencing the expression finally given by the Convention to its views on the subject of the incorporation of the Territories in the proposed Union. It is typical of the general outlook at that period that the view taken of the principle of incorporation paid little attention to the feeling entertained on the subject by the inhabitants of the Territories concerned. It is clear, nevertheless, that there could in fact have been no doubt regarding the view taken by Natives in the Territories, for some of the Chiefs concerned had lost no time in showing that they were strongly opposed to any such measure. The Basuto, who had had their experience of rule by Cape Colony, sent a deputation to England which asked for an assurance that their country should not be incorporated in the projected Union.[5] They asked that if this were inevitable, then the existing form of Native Government should remain, and that the land should be reserved entirely for Basuto use and should be inalienable. They were told in reply by the Secretary of State that there would be no immediate change, but that if South Africa were to be united, then it would be desirable, as well as necessary, for the Basuto to be prepared to come some day under the same Government as the rest of South Africa. If so, arrangements would be made that the land should be reserved for the use of the Basuto, the sale of liquor should be prohibited, and the National Council of Basutoland should be retained. Nor was there any room for doubt as to the attitude of the Bechuana Chiefs on the question of incorporation. On the publication of Lord Selborne's Memorandum, a protest had been sent to him by a group headed by Lentswe,[6] Chief of the Kgotla, who had a reputation as one of the most experienced and at the same time most progressive Chiefs of his time. It was in connexion with this protest that the High Commissioner, in the course of a subsequent visit to Mafeking early in 1910, informed the Chiefs that the transfer for which provision had been made in the Union Act of 1909 would not take place in the immediate future. It was, he added, impossible to say how long it might be before Bechuanaland was handed over, 'but in the natural course of things it would take place some day'.[7]

Though it became clear in the course of discussion in the Convention that there was a general agreement as to the desirability of incorporating the Territories in the Union, the known attitude of the British Government as declared in

---

[5] Sir G. Lagden, *The Basuto* (1909), p. 620, and *Annual Report, Basutoland, 1908–9*, p. 4.
[6] *Native Administration*, Pt. V, p. 207; Sillery, op cit., p. 157.
[7] Colonial Reports (Bechuanaland), No. 652 (1909–10), p. 12.

1906, combined with the standing cleavage of principle between the delegates in regard to the enfranchisement of Natives, seemed to prevent the Convention joining in any definite recommendation to this effect. In his history of the Convention, of which he himself was a member, Sir E. H. Walton writes:

> It was necessary to remember that the assent of the Imperial Government would only be given [to legislation creating the Union] if the special trust it held with regard to the Natives were duly safeguarded. . . . It was certainly desirable that these Territories should be included in the Union for administrative purposes . . . [but] the Native peoples must find in the Constitution such provision for their protection and for their interests that they would be induced of their own free will to be included in the new State about to be created.

On the other hand, as he says, it seemed highly undesirable that the urgent problems created by inter-state antagonisms should have to wait for a practical means of solution until agreement could be reached on these questions of principle.[8]

The delegates decided therefore to place in the forefront of the recommendations to the British Parliament a scheme designed to secure with the least possible delay a legislative union adequate to deal with the pressing problems created by inter-state rivalries, and for the rest to make proposals calculated to forestall such difficulties as could be foreseen regarding the enfranchisement of Africans or the system of Native administration to be followed in the event of the incorporation of the High Commission Territories in the Union. But the form to be taken by these proposals gave rise to long and contentious discussions. The Cape Colony delegates argued strenuously in favour of a provision for the general extension of the system of Native franchise which was part of the constitution of their own Colony. In this, however, they failed, and the opposition from the North to the principle of Native enfranchisement became so strong as to make them fear that

[8] Sir E. H. Walton, *The Inner History of the National Convention of South Africa* (Maskew Miller, 1912), pp. 294-5.

the existing provision made by Cape legislation in favour of Natives might be jeopardized when the Union came into being. To safeguard its future, therefore, they succeeded in securing a provision which entrenched it behind the requirement of a two-thirds majority of both Houses of the Union Parliament in support of any change.[9] The safeguards for the High Commission Territories in the event of their transfer to the Union took the form of providing guarantees regarding their lands, their tribal institutions, and the liquor traffic. These safeguards were to be secured of practical effect by the institution of a special procedure of Native Administration under direct control of the Governor-General in Council. This was a proposal which caused exceptional difficulty.[10] It was criticized as tending to take the final authority out of the hands of the Union Parliament and subject it to the decision of an agent of the Imperial Parliament. It became necessary for the High Commissioner, who had already reminded the Chairman of the weight attached by the British Government to its obligations to the tribes, to add now, in an even more forcible letter, a reminder that 'it is no question of policy that we are discussing; it is a question of honour, and one in which every section of public opinion in the United Kingdom, Government and Opposition alike, is keenly sensitive'.

The final decision to include these provisions represented a compromise which was effected with difficulty, and it did not fail to meet with some of the obstacles anticipated by the Convention when its delegation brought to England the draft Bill in which it was embodied. There were in Parliament many members of the Conservative Party who had opposed in 1906 the concession of Responsible Government to the two Boer Republics. There were on the other hand many of their opponents who, while proud of that measure as a proof of the vitality of Liberal doctrine, looked askance when they learned that they would be unable to insist that the new Union should reproduce in the two Northern Republics the liberal franchise which was in force in the Cape. They were even more

[9] Section 152, Act of Union 1909. [10] Thompson, op. cit., p. 274 ff.

concerned when they were informed that in the Cape itself this measure must actually be protected by the device of the 'entrenched clause', if it was to be maintained against attacks emanating from Afrikaner quarters.

In the circumstances it was not unnatural that the Government should be hard pressed in Parliament in regard to the provisions in the Bill which would regulate the transfer of the three Territories to the new Union. It was necessary for the Government spokesman to emphasize that the provision for transfer was intended to be merely permissive.

> The Schedule [he said] . . . does not bring transfer one hour nearer. In fact, in so far as it goes, I think it will be conclusively proved that it makes it somewhat more difficult. . . . If the Bill passes . . . and it comes into full operation, in the long distant years it well may be when these Protectorates are transferred, . . . you will have the transition so gradual that I hope and believe that the natives will never know from anything that occurs to them that the transition has been effected.[11]

As regards the constitutional sanctions required for the act of transfer, the Prime Minister, Mr. Asquith, argued that

> the important point is that you cannot bring any one of these Protectorates or Territories into a state of subordination to the Union Government or the Union Parliament, as Clause 151 shows, unless the King, with the advice of the Privy Council, that is, the Cabinet here, agrees. That is a most proper recognition on the part of the South African communities that the Imperial Government has a voice, and the ultimate voice, in relation to this matter.[12]

Whether or not the Prime Minister was warranted in suggesting that the obligation which lay on the King to obtain the advice of his Privy Council necessarily implied that the assent of Parliament itself was essential for the act of cession, it is nevertheless true that no British Minister could venture to advise the Crown to take such a step without the certainty that it would carry the support of Parliament.

At the committee stage the Under Secretary of State for

[11] Cmd. 8707, p. 115.   [12] Ibid., p. 116.

the Colonies repeated that he had already given, with the sanction of the Prime Minister, the pledge that, in regard to transfer, 'so far as we could bind ourselves and our successors, no such action would be taken without the House of Commons being informed'. Questioned on this latter point, he explained that before any transfer took place the House would 'have the opportunity of discussing, and, if they wish, of disapproving of the action of the Government'. He added the important statement that 'It would, I know, meet the views of some of my Honourable Friends if we were to say the consent of all the natives must be obtained, but, apart from that technical point, I can assure the House that the wishes of the natives in the territories will be most carefully considered before any transfer takes place.'[13]

In the House of Lords Lord Crewe, speaking as Secretary of State for the Colonies, repeated that as trustee for the interests of the Natives of the Territories, the Government had decided to ask the Legislatures in South Africa to accept the provisions for transfer embodied in the Schedule. They had been accepted with very slight amendment.[14] He went on to say:

Here I may say that we have no desire, we are in no hurry, to hand over these areas to anyone. They are contented, they are not otherwise than prosperous, and we have no desire to part with them; in fact, they have expressed themselves as averse to passing from under the direct administration of the Crown. But . . . it does not seem conceivable that for an indefinite future these areas should remain administered from here and that the new South African Union should have no lot or part on their administration. Nor do I believe . . . that it is possible to name a time limit and say, at any rate, we will not hand over a particular area for a fixed number of years . . . you cannot combine that provision in the Bill with the existence of the terms embodied in the Schedule, because although we do not desire to hand over the Protectorates, yet the existence of the Schedule

---

[13] Ibid., p. 116. For a precedent for the consultation of a Native people before transfer to another Administration, see p. 20 above.

[14] Thompson, op. cit., p. 416 ff.; Walton, op. cit., p. 321 ff.

undoubtedly contemplates their being possibly handed over at some time to be fixed by agreement.

In regard to the addition of the Schedule to the Act, he added,

What weighs with me as much as anything is that the natives themselves are not anxious to be transferred, but, admitting that they may be some day transferred, actively desire the incorporation of a charter such as this in the Act itself.[15]

The South Africa Act, 1909, was passed with only a few verbal alterations in Section 151 and in the Schedule as approved by the National Convention. It had received its second reading in a 'practically empty' House of Commons.[16] It may indeed seem strange that a measure which left the disposal of the principle of the Native franchise to the vote of the Union Parliament should have passed so easily through the Imperial Parliament of that day. True, the draft Act of Union had been brought forward when the attention of the British Parliament was absorbed in the struggle between the Government and the House of Lords over the Lloyd George budget. But the Liberal Government which had taken so strong a stand on the question in 1906 was still in full command. W. P. Schreiner, devoted to the cause of the Cape franchise, had carried to England the case against the Afrikaner insistence on a political colour bar, and had vigorously canvassed there the case for the extension of the Cape franchise.[17] There was within the Liberal Party itself a section which deplored the apparent insecurity of the Cape franchise; even the Prime Minister, Mr. Asquith, was driven to declare that on this point there seemed to be no difference of opinion in Great Britain. But, he argued, the Bill must be passed without amendment. 'It was either the measure as it stood or no Union at all.' In effect, the failure to insist on the extension of the Cape franchise was a concession to Afrikaner opinion, and though this was not fully apparent at the time, it was in due course to

---

[15] Cmd. 8707, p. 117.
[16] *Cambridge History of the British Empire*, loc. cit., p. 374.
[17] Thompson, op. cit., p. 402 ff.

have its corollary in strengthening the Afrikaner demand for the incorporation of the three Territories in the Union.

Turning, however, now to those incidents in the debate on the Bill which were of more immediate concern to the High Commission Territories, it may be said that nothing has since occurred either in the course of British legislation or in the form of ministerial statements which would affect in any way the validity of the undertakings given by the Government in 1909. The pledge regarding the process of 'consultation' with the Natives (the term which now came into general use) was repeated by Ministers in statements made to the House of Commons in 1919 and 1925. In 1925 Lord Onslow told the House of Lords that the Government would not come to any decisions regarding a transfer, until both the Native and the White population had had full opportunity of expressing their views, and that any representations which either might make to His Majesty's Government would receive the most careful consideration before it came to any final decision. In 1923 the Secretary of State for the Colonies emphasized to a deputation from Swaziland that his object in permitting it to address him was to implement this undertaking by giving the people of Swaziland an opportunity of expressing their views personally to him. In 1954 Sir Winston Churchill, dealing as Prime Minister with the argument advanced by the Union Government that the completion of the Union's programme for defence was dependent on the early transfer to it of the three High Commission Territories, reminded Dr. Malan that before this could take place their inhabitants had first to be consulted.[18]

On one or two occasions it has been suggested that these pledges had the force of a provision that any transfer of the Territories must have the prior consent of their inhabitants. There is, however, no warrant for such a suggestion. The Parliamentary Committee which met in 1934 to consider the constitutional position regarding the three Territories which

[18] Walker, op. cit., p. 912.

had arisen from the passing of the Statute of Westminster in
1931 made the following remarks on this subject.

H.M.G. of Great Britain have never adopted the position that they
will not transfer the territories unless the inhabitants of these
territories consent to transfer, but they have definitely promised
those inhabitants that they shall be heard on the subject, and that
any representations they may make shall be duly considered.[19]

[19] Cmd. 8707, p. 134.

III

RELATIONS AFTER THE
ACT OF 1909

WITH the passing of the Act of 1909 the relations of the High
Commission Territories with the Union moved into a new
phase. Looking back at their earlier history, their people had
been obliged to face the acquisitive approach of settlers who
were on some occasions of British and on others of Afrikaner
origin, with differing ideologies in respect of the rights of
Africans. But it is not certain that the people of the Territories
had in fact had good reason to see a marked difference between
them. A quarter of a century before the meeting of the
National Convention of 1907, when the Basuto were still under
the administration of the Cape Government, it had made an
announcement which showed that the attitude of a predomi-
nantly British administration could be no less predatory than
that of the Afrikaner leaders in the Transvaal or the Orange
Free State. It announced that as soon as it had quelled the
resistance shown by Morosi, one of the major Basuto Chiefs,
against the decree of disarmament, his district (Quthing)
would be taken over and opened to occupation by European
settlers.[1] The Bechuanaland Chiefs were not likely to forget
that the British Colonial Office had in 1895 made no secret of
its determination to hand over the administration of the
Bechuanaland Protectorate to the Chartered Company,[2] thus
presenting them with the unhappy prospect that a large part
of their lands, like those of Matabeleland lying immediately
to their north, might forthwith be taken over for colonization
by European settlers. They were in some measure saved from
this fate by the persistence and resolution of the four Chiefs
who visited England in 1895, though at the cost of the

[1] *Native Administration*, Pt. V, p. 51.   [2] Sillery, op. cit., p. 65 ff.

surrender to the Chartered Company of a considerable area of land lying along the route of its Rhodesian Railway. It was left for the ill-omened dispatch of the Jameson Raid to give the final blow to the proposal to hand over the control of the whole Protectorate to the Chartered Company.[3] As an historian of the Protectorate afterwards wrote, 'one cannot read of these events without some embarrassment'. It is no less disturbing to realize that some years later, when the delegates were on the point of gathering for the National Convention, delegates from Natal and the Orange Colony were asking for power to take up Native lands in exchange for others in Bechuanaland, and that some of the Cape members sought to annexe the fertile lands in the southern strip of the Protectorate even before the transfer of the Territory as a whole to the Union.[4] The strength of this movement was shortly to be seen when the Natal delegation formally registered its vote against Clause 14 in the draft Schedule which aimed at prohibiting the alienation of land in Basutoland or of lands forming part of the Native Reserve in the other two Territories.[5] Their attitude was not in fact very far different from that of the Boer leaders in the Transvaal in 1904 who, faced with the problem of a shortage of labour, had advocated that 'Basutoland and Swaziland and the Reserves should be broken up and the squatters law strictly enforced to secure an equal distribution of labourers'.[6]

With the passing of the Act of Union the three Territories had henceforth to deal with a Government representing four component States, which was less likely to yield to the influence of local pressure groups, and was moreover committed to respect the provisions of Section 151 of the Union Act, designed to safeguard the land and other rights of the Native inhabitants of the Territories. As stated by Lord Crewe in the House of Lords, the clauses of the Bill embodying these provisions had been put before the four Legislatures in South Africa and had been accepted by them.[7]

---

[3] See p. 53 below.   [4] Walker, op. cit., p. 535.
[5] Walton, op. cit., p. 301.   [6] Walker, op. cit., p. 511.
[7] See p. 35 above.

For some years after the passing of the Act no proposal for incorporation of the Territories came forward, and the record of their relations with the Union is confined to matters which, though of some concern to them, were no longer of such critical interest. The operation of the Customs Union,[8] of which they had been members since 1903, involved negotiations which at first seemed to present complications of some difficulty. They were solved by the adoption of a formula which eventually gave to Basutoland a fixed percentage of 0·88575 per cent. of the total customs receipts of the whole customs area,[9] and Bechuanaland 0·2762 per cent.[10] A similar procedure was followed in the case of Swaziland, which after some initial variations finally received 0·149 per cent. of the whole customs receipts.[11] Nor does any trouble seem to have arisen in earlier years over a matter which was perhaps of more vital concern to the Native people of the High Commission Territories, namely the supply of 'migrant labour' to the Union. This has formed in different degrees one of the major sources of subsistence for the people of the Territories; it has indeed been described as the 'balancing factor' in the economy of Basutoland. There the census of 1956 showed 154,782 as the number of males and females absent outside the Territory, 'mostly migrant workers'. The Agricultural Survey of the Territory published in 1952 estimated that the persons absent from their villages at any one time (nearly all working in the Union) numbered 77,000 males and 22,000 females. This amounted very roughly to between 50 per cent. and 60 per cent. of the able-bodied workers. The Basuto had a high reputation in the Union mines as shaft-sinkers. In 1959 it was stated that 40,757 were employed in the gold mines and 55,119 in all mines in the Union. It was estimated in 1950 that the average credit made by 'migrant' labour to the resources of the Territory amounted to between £375,000 and £400,000 a year. There has not

---

[8] Walker, op. cit., p. 507.
[9] *Annual Report, Basutoland, 1910–11*, p. 14.
[10] *Annual Report, Bechuanaland, 1959*, p. 16.
[11] *Annual Report, Swaziland, 1959*, p. 28.

been the same ratio of migration from the Bechuanaland
Protectorate. A careful investigation made in 1938–40
estimated that some 27·5 per cent. of the adult males of the
Protectorate were away from home; they came mainly from
the eastern side of the Territory, which contains the greater
proportion of the population, and it was estimated that one-
third to one-half of the able-bodied manpower of those districts
was normally away from home at one time, while perhaps
70 or 80 per cent. had either been abroad or were still absent.
Their natural destination is the Union. In 1958, some 21,598
workers were shown as having left the Territory for the Union.
They are reported to have brought back £298,635 to the
Territory.[12] Migration from Swaziland has been a less prominent factor, for among the Swazi the scale of indigenous
subsistence is far higher than in the other two Territories.
Estimates have placed at about 25 to 30 per cent. the proportion of able-bodied Swazi who are away at any one time from
their homes.[13] In 1959, a total of 7,912 Swazi were recruited
by the two major recruiting organizations for work in the
mines of the Rand and Natal, and it was estimated that between
3,000 and 4,000 Swazi found other employment in the
districts of the Union which border the Territory.

But if the 'migrant labour' is a useful asset to the Territories,
a supply of imported African manpower has also been vital
to the industrial life of the Union. An interdepartmental committee on labour resources spoke in 1930 of the Union's
'chronic shortage of labour'. It is not possible to say with
accuracy what proportion of the total labour force of the
Union, estimated at 2,240,000 in all, is actually indigenous,
but there are certain facts which throw some light on the
relative part taken by 'foreign' labour. In 1946, only 41·25 per
cent. of the 305,410 African workers employed in the industries
represented in the Witwatersrand Native Labour Association
had had their homes within the Union. In 1954 it was stated
by the Tomlinson Commission that some 650,000 Native

[12] *Annual Report, Bechuanaland, 1959*, p. 33.
[13] *An African Survey*, p. 1380.

workers came from beyond the borders of the Union.[14] Of the great body of non-indigenous labour in the Union the three High Commission Territories have admittedly supplied only a minor part. In 1945 and the neighbouring years the gold mines on the Rand were said to draw 140,000 of their Native labourers from the Union, 50,000 from the High Commission Territories, 80,000 from Portuguese Mozambique, and 25,000 from the tropical North.[15] But the fact that labour from the Territories is near at hand, and therefore does not require acclimatizing, adds to its value. As will subsequently be shown, the Union Government has in the past been for various reasons under pressure to restrict labour immigration from the Territories, but up to 1960, at all events, regulations seem to have tended to come rather from the Administrations in the Territories, such as rules limiting the supply of manpower available to the recruiting agencies working from the Union, or those prescribing the period for which labour can enlist for service in the Union, or those providing means for ensuring its return.[16] These regulations have been made rather to secure good working conditions than actually to restrict the flow of labour. With the exception of a rule affecting the employment of High Commission labour in Scheduled Town areas, there seem to have been in the past no labour regulations of any importance issued from the Union which specifically affected immigrant labour from the Territories as apart from that coming from other external sources. In a memorandum drawn up in 1939 by the Union Government it was stated that

as extra-Union Natives are continually entering the Union in large numbers without permission, a provision was included in Act No. 46 of 1937 making it an offence for any 'foreign' Native to enter [the Union] or for any European to employ such Native in any town within the Union without special permission from the Secretary for Native Affairs. This restriction does not, however, apply to the Natives of the Territories or of South-West Africa, as the future of

[14] U.G. 61/1955, Pretoria, p. 41.
[15] Walker, op. cit., p. 754.
[16] *An African Survey*, p. 1408.

these areas has thus far been regarded as being more intimately associated with the Union. For the same reason the restriction imposed by the Union's Immigration Laws upon the entry of any person from outside the Union, be he European or Native, have not been applied to the Territories.[17]

As will subsequently be shown,[18] this aspect of the immigration law has been materially altered by the legislation of 1962 which reflects the more recent attitude of the Republic in the matter. It is of some interest to add that the regulation of 1914 suspending recruitment of labour north of latitude 22 degrees south was due to the impression that labour coming from the tropics was specially liable to suffer from either miners' silicosis or tuberculosis.[19] But this did not affect recruitment from Basutoland or Swaziland, and it applied only to that part of Bechuanaland which lies north of the Tropic of Capricorn.

If there was anything in the past history of relations of this character which may be said to have caused a sense of tension, it was to be found rather in the measures taken by the Union which affected the export of livestock from the Territories. This export was of great importance to Bechuanaland in particular, but both that Territory and Basutoland suffered from the regulation excluding light-weight cattle from sale in the Union.[20] That was a measure which was resented as having been passed in the interest of European farmers, and in the course of correspondence carried on in 1937 General Hertzog seems to have admitted that such was in fact the case. 'Union cattle farmers',[21] he said, 'could be placated in this matter [i.e. the removal of restriction on the sale of light-weight cattle] only if the Union Government were placed in a position to use the argument that the relaxation of these restrictions is an exigency arising out of the transfer of the Territories.' A similar argument would no doubt have been applied to the current complaints about the application of the system of quotas to

[17] Cmd. 8707, p. 101. [18] See p. 112 below. [19] *An African Survey*, p. 1406.
[20] Tshekedi Khama, *Bechuanaland and South Africa* (Africa Bureau, 1955), p. 15.
[21] Cmd. 8707, p. 85.

the export of agricultural produce from the Territories, though
in this instance the effect was probably far less restrictive.
Both Bechuanaland and Basutoland also had cause for complaint because export of cattle to the Union had on occasion
been barred by vigorous precautions against the spread of
foot-and-mouth disease, the more so as they have on occasion
coincided with a period of acute price depression.[22] It was not
unnatural for the sufferers to suspect that such regulations
were being enforced for political rather than hygienic reasons;[23]
but it is fair to note here that restrictions of this nature have
been applied not merely to the Territories, but to exports from
Rhodesia, South West Africa, and the Transkeian area of the
Union.

The eastern and more populous parts of the Bechuanaland
Protectorate have had the benefit of the services of the
Rhodesian Railway, which carries on from Mafeking to Southern Rhodesia the Union railway line starting from Cape Town.
The length of line in the Protectorate was constructed through
the agency of the British South Africa Company at the period
when it had been denied access to Matabeleland through the
Transvaal. In 1945 the shares in the Rhodesian Railway were
purchased by the Government of Southern Rhodesia and
assigned to a statutory authority of which the High Commissioner of the three High Commission Territories was until
recently a member; in 1953 its operation became the responsibility of the Federation of Rhodesia and Nyasaland. Of the
total length of track, there are 1,356 miles in Southern
Rhodesia, 643 in Northern Rhodesia, 399 in the Bechuanaland
Protectorate, and 112 in the Union. The administration of
the length of line from Mahalapye to Ramaquabane, formerly
conducted by the Union, was in 1959 taken over by the
Rhodesian Railways. To this extent, therefore, the Union had
only a minor share in the operation of this railway.[24]

There was, however, at one time a possibility that the

[22] Walker, op. cit., p. 661; Sillery, op. cit., p. 99.
[23] Perham and Curtis, op. cit., p. 51 ff.
[24] *An African Survey*, p. 1552.

Union might possess a controlling share in a line which was explicitly designed to serve the special needs of the Protectorate. Not long after the passing of the Act of Union, plans began to be mooted for a railway taking off from near Matetsi in Southern Rhodesia and running westward to join up with the South West Africa railway system near Gobabis. From there it would eventually find its terminus at Walvis Bay, with the result that some 594 miles would lie in the Protectorate, and 440 in South West Africa. The project offered to the Union the strategic value of a direct access to the Atlantic seaboard. For the Bechuanaland Protectorate it opened the possibility of a new market for the export of Bechuana cattle. But it is obvious that it could not have been constructed without the active co-operation of the Government of the Union, and it was made clear that this would not be forthcoming. Apart from other considerations it was obvious that there was little prospect of adequate traffic returns for a line which would be expensive both to construct and to maintain.[25]

The position and area of Basutoland and Swaziland do not give them the same importance as Bechuanaland in regard to schemes for a wide extension of the Union railway system. In Basutoland the provision of roadways has been restricted by the difficulties of a mountainous terrain, and there has been only one mile of railway connecting Maseru to Marseilles on the Bloemfontein-Natal line. But a systematic provision for passenger and goods traffic in Swaziland has been established by the Motor Services of the Union State Railways. As will be shown subsequently, the possibility of a transfer of Swaziland was being seriously considered by the British and Union Governments during the year 1926,[26] and attention was then drawn to the prospect that an extension of the Union system would, with little additional cost, both open up to Swaziland the coal resources of the Transvaal and provide a new line of communication with the coast. It had been admitted in 1919 that the Union Government would not move in the matter

[25] *Native Administration*, Pt. V, p. 158; Walker, op. cit., p. 913.
[26] See p. 58 ff. below.

'while Swaziland was still an administration independent of it', but it was stated in 1926 by the Prime Minister of the Union that it could be regarded as reasonably certain that a railway would be constructed 'as soon as possible after transfer . . . to the Union takes place'.[27] Some reference will subsequently be made[28] to a recent scheme, not calling for the participation of the Union, which will provide Swaziland with direct rail connexion to the sea coast.

It should be added here that for a considerable number of years, the Union Post Office administered the postal and telegraph services in Swaziland and controlled the posts, but not the telegraphs, of Bechuanaland.[29] It has also been of great advantage to all three of the Territories that the currency of the Union has been full legal tender in them. This has rendered possible the extension of banking facilities to all three Territories.

It may be convenient to mention here, too, a scheme which soon after the passing of the Act of Union caused the public of the Cape to take a special interest in the Bechuanaland Protectorate. This arose from the publication of the theories advanced by Professor Schwartz regarding the origin of the Okavango Swamp area, which extends to about 4,000 square miles in the north of the Protectorate. He held that the swamp had at some remote period taken the place of a vast series of inland lakes which had dried up owing to a chain of fluvial dislocations in the rivers that had once fed them. A suitable treatment of the Zambezi riverain would, in his view, recreate the lake system, with a resulting improvement in the atmospheric conditions which influence the humidity of the Cape. Though other scientists did not give their support to these speculations, the scheme held for many years a vivid interest for the farming community in the Cape, and there were many who urged the Union Government to acquire an early incorporation of the Protectorate in the Union, in order to forestall

---

[27] Cmd. 8707, p. 25.   [28] See pp. 110–11.
[29] This position was materially modified in 1960 and 1961 but the details are of no great interest.

any obstacles created by the Administration of the Protectorate, which, they argued, had not the same reason to appreciate the benefits held out by the scheme. That interest survived for many years, and as late as 1945 the Union Government secured the co-operation of the Protectorate Administration in promoting an expedition to explore any possibilities which the Okavango Delta might offer for the use of modern engineering methods.[30] The investigations of the expedition, however, cast doubt on the data used by Professor Schwartz in support of his theory, though they proved of value in carrying out a minor adjustment in the drainage system.[31]

There existed a considerable measure of contact at various levels between the Administrations of the three Territories and the scientific and administrative services of the Union Government. As was pointed out by the Joint Advisory Committee on Co-operation in 1939,[32] the technical services of geologists, engineers, and scientific workers, particularly in the field of agriculture and animal health, were from time to time placed at the disposal of the Territories by the Union departments. There was in particular a common policy on operations dealing with locust and tsetse fly, and in Bechuanaland the cost of control measures undertaken in areas adjoining the Union border were shared by the two Governments. There was also co-operation in measures taken for control of malaria. In some cases representatives of the Territories had a part in the management of the Union Boards exercising control over local products. The inhabitants of the Territories were able to receive their education in higher standards at schools in the Union, paying the ordinary fees. Basutoland in particular was able to send students to the South Africa Native College at Fort Hare,[33] towards maintenance of which the High Commission Territories made an annual grant. In 1950, for political reasons, the College was closed to students from

---

[30] *An African Survey*, pp. 982–4; Walker, op. cit., p. 913.
[31] See the 'Morse Report', more fully entitled *Basutoland, Bechuanaland Protectorate and Swaziland. Report of an Economic Survey Mission* (H.M.S.O., 1960).
[32] Cmd. 8707, p. 91.   [33] *An African Survey*, pp. 1141–2.

non-Union areas, and this caused considerable feeling in
Basutoland. In 1953, however, the protests of this Territory
secured an alteration of policy, and non-Union students
were again admitted.

It has been convenient to allow this account of the relations
between the Territories and the Union to proceed somewhat
beyond the year 1913, when the Union Ministers first made
their efforts to persuade the British Government to agree to
the transfer of the administration of the Territories to the
Union. But as will be seen in the following section, this phase
was for the most part limited to correspondence between the
Union Ministers and the Ministers of the Crown in Great
Britain, and it had for many years little direct effect on the
character of the local relations between the Territories and the
Union.

IV

EFFORTS BY THE UNION TO SECURE INCORPORATION

THESE efforts began with the approach made by General
Botha in 1913, and for many subsequent years they involved
an almost continuous exchange of correspondence. The record
of these exchanges will reveal a gradual change of attitude on
both sides. As has been seen, the British Government had in
1909 made it clear that it was its purpose to transfer the
administration of the Territories to the Union, after a process
of consultation with their inhabitants on the question of
transfer; it had, however, been careful to avoid giving to the
Union any definite pledge of transfer, or assigning any date
when this might take place, and had been equally careful to
avoid a pledge to their Native peoples that transfer would not
take place unless they themselves had assented to it. But the
British Government had not foreseen the degree to which it
might come to be influenced by the attitude of the British
public regarding the policy pursued by the Government of the
Union in regard to the position to be allowed to the African
people in the political and social life of the Union itself. In
1909 the British had anticipated that with the consummation
of the Union, the traditional attitude of the Northern States
on this question would be progressively influenced by contact
with the more liberal views then held in the Cape. There had,
for example, been something almost pathetic in the faith
shown by some members of the National Convention in the
certainty of the survival of the franchise system of the Cape
against any attacks that might come from the less liberal
members of the new Union Parliament. It was impossible,
one of them said, 'to find a single instance when a great
body of persons . . ., a whole race, has been disfranchised in

democratic times'.[1] But these anticipations were not justified by the course of events, and in proportion as the attitude of the more influential party in Union politics hardened, the views held by British authorities on the propriety of the transfer of the Territories also underwent a definite change. The Native peoples of the Territories remained consistently opposed to their incorporation in the Union, but the opposition of the Native peoples to transfer did not in truth form a decisive factor in the British attitude on the subject, or at all events was never put forward as such. If the British Ministers found it convenient to lay emphasis on the necessity of prior 'consultation' with the African people of the Territories, it is clearly because they considered this to provide a more politic form of reply than an open condemnation of the Native policy known to be held by the majority of voters in the Union.

The Union Government on its side will also be seen to have varied its line of approach to the question of transfer. At the outset, it preferred to assume that the indications given by the British of their intention to transfer the Territories were equivalent to a definite undertaking to accept such proposals as the Union might put forward to this effect, providing that the Union undertook on its part to observe the provisions of the Schedule in the Act intended to safeguard the interests of the Natives of the Territories after transfer. It proved easy for the British Government to establish that there had in fact been no explicit undertaking of this nature, and for a short time this answer served its purpose, and when the Union Ministers renewed their approach with growing insistence, they were driven to support their case by arguments based on the current relations between the Territories and the Union which were either fallacious or of very little real substance. Why then did the Union Ministers persist in renewing with increasing insistence what had started as friendly appeals, but were to assume progressively the aspect of imperative demands carrying almost the aspect of threats? One cannot avoid the conclusion that the dominant motive was the resentment

[1] Perham and Curtis, op. cit., p. 14.

caused by the implied repudiation of the Native policy of the Union. If incorporation were refused, the three Territories would constitute a physical enclave to which the Native policy of the majority party in the Union could not be applied. Until the Union could secure their incorporation under its own administration they would therefore remain as a standing argument against that policy and the ideology which underlay it.

It is no doubt this aspect of the issue that accounts for the fact that such approaches as were made were put forward by individual Ministers of the Union, and never actually took the form of an address to the Crown from the Houses of Parliament of the Union, which at all events up to 1931, the date of the passing of the Statute of Westminster, formed the procedure prescribed for securing the incorporation of the Territories.

The first approach was, as has been stated, made by General Botha in a letter dated 12 March 1913, addressed to Lord Gladstone, as High Commissioner in South Africa.[2] General Botha had made in the Union House of Assembly a reference to the position in regard to the three Territories, and now explained that he took the opportunity of referring again to that statement in view of the allusion made by Sir Starr Jameson in the course of a recent Annual Meeting of the Chartered Company, since this bore a reference to the development of Bechuanaland. But there was in fact nothing in Sir Starr Jameson's address which need have caused disquiet to General Botha. There was never any secret that when the British South Africa Company received its Charter in 1889, Bechuanaland had been included within the widely-drawn field of its activities. For various reasons Matabeleland and Mashonaland had in the first instance been taken under its direct administration, but in 1894 Cecil Rhodes, anxious to clarify the position regarding the section of the Rhodesian railway which ran through the Protectorate, approached the British Colonial Office with a request that Bechuanaland

[2] Cmd. 8707, p. 12.

should now be brought under the direct administration of the Company. He received a favourable reply.[3] As already shown above,[4] the area of the Protectorate which was to become known as British Bechuanaland was formally annexed to Cape Colony early in 1895, and Rhodes took early in that year the opportunity of mentioning to the Cape Assembly the grounds for the proposal to transfer the rest of the area of the Protectorate to the administration of the Chartered Company.[5] As a preliminary measure, the Colonial Office transferred in October 1895 the administration of the Malete and Rolong tribal areas of the Protectorate to the Company, but when in the following December the 'Jameson Raid' set out from Pitsani in the Protectorate, the Colonial Office started to have second thoughts as to the desirability of the transfer of the rest of the Protectorate, and the Company was warned by a letter of 18 January 1896 that the proposed transfer 'must stand over for the present'. The Proclamation which had transferred the Malete and Rolong areas to its administration was cancelled in a Proclamation of 3 February 1896.

It is true that in 1897 Rhodes was able to claim that though the actual transfer of the Protectorate to the administration of the Company had been postponed *sine die* in 1895, the undertaking to make the transfer still subsisted, and this view was apparently accepted when the Southern Rhodesia Order in Council of 1898 reproduced a clause of the original Matabeleland Order which empowered the Secretary of State to include the Protectorate within the jurisdiction of the Chartered Company. Nevertheless, it is not easy to see how Sir Starr Jameson could have seriously entertained in 1913 a hope that the power conferred on the Secretary of State in 1895 would now be exercised in favour of the Company. Nor indeed does it seem that he actually introduced the mention of the Protectorate in his speech with a view to encouraging any such hope. He was in fact discussing the three alternative courses which might be taken in regard to the areas in Matabeleland and Mashonaland then administered by the Company when its

[3] Sillery, op. cit., p. 66 ff.   [4] See p. 9.   [5] Walker, op. cit., p. 446 ff.

Charter came to be terminated, these alternatives being inclusion in the Union, or recognition as a Crown Colony, or the grant of Responsible Government. He regarded the second alternative as immeasurably the least desirable, and he quoted the stagnation of Bechuanaland as an illustration of what the normal Crown Colony could look like. 'In all its considerable length of railway line', he remarked, 'it has not a single railway station or even a single siding.' That, he added, was the present position, but there was always a possibility that some day 'the Company might make a change for the better in Bechuanaland when it came into its inheritance'.

He did not proceed to suggest how that eventually might come about nor what form it might take. It seems indeed that General Botha's reference to the Chartered Company and to Bechuanaland served mainly to furnish him with a suitable opportunity for the approach he now desired to make to the question of incorporation of the High Commission Territories in the Union. There was no question, Botha said, that it was contemplated at the time of the Act of Union that all the Protectorates, sooner or later, would be transferred to the Union. He considered that the Union 'must now press for the transfer, at the earliest possible date, of Swaziland and at the same time of Bechuanaland', but he added: 'Should the simultaneous transfer of both these Protectorates not be feasible in the opinion of the Imperial Government, then we urge that Bechuanaland also be transferred as soon as possible after the incorporation of Swaziland has been settled.'[6]

General Botha was informed that the question of the transfer of Swaziland might be considered,[7] but the High Commissioner was authorized in a dispatch dated 2 May 1913 to explain to him that it would not be possible in the near future to justify to Parliament a proposal for transferring the Protectorate. It seems obvious that the Secretary of State, in giving these directions to the High Commissioner, was embarrassed to find any definite reason for discrimination between Swaziland and Bechuanaland. The dispatch mentions

[6] Cmd. 8707, pp. 12–13.   [7] Ibid., p. 6.

indeed that 'alike in history and actual conditions the Protectorate differs greatly from Swaziland'. But in order to justify his decision regarding Bechuanaland, he had to fall back on the plea that the Chartered Company had acquired certain commercial and industrial rights in the Protectorate, including the right to acquire further concessions of the same order. There was, he said, no intention whatever of handing over the administration of the Protectorate to the Chartered Company, but he implied that the existence of these concessions would make it difficult to transfer the Protectorate to the Union. General Botha might well have questioned the logic of this argument, had not the correspondence been broken off by the outbreak of the First World War in 1914.

After the end of the war, General Botha took up the correspondence again at the point at which it had left off. Acting on the admission that Swaziland might be considered for transfer, he now sent to Lord Milner, who had succeeded Mr. L. Harcourt as Secretary of State, a carefully reasoned statement of the grounds on which he sought the agreement of the British Government to carry out this measure.[8] The war, he said, had left the Union immensely stronger than before, and it had received an extension of its area and responsibilities through the grant of the Mandate for South West Africa. There was, he added, no special urgency about the transfer of Basutoland or Bechuanaland, though as soon as the inclusion of Rhodesia in the Union (a possibility for which provision had been made in Section 150 of the Act of Union) had become a practical question, the transfer of Bechuanaland would have to be dealt with. Swaziland, he pointed out, was in a different position from the other two Territories. Before the Boer War it had been administered by the Transvaal. It was not an exclusively Native Territory, but contained 'a fair White population consisting mainly of old Transvaal residents'. An immediate transfer was called for, as this would supply the Union with valuable experience to guide it in the eventual administration of the other Territories. It would also enable it

[8] Memorandum accompanying letter of 2 July 1919 (Cmd. 8707, p. 14).

to make better provision for the political representation of the resident White population in Swaziland. They were now in a somewhat anomalous position, but it was the intention of the Union to provide full political and parliamentary rights and privileges for them. Lastly, transfer would enable the Union to spend money on various developments now badly needed in Swaziland, and in particular on the railway required to make available for it the coal resources of the Transvaal. There is evidence that while Generals Botha and Smuts were in England they discussed this memorandum with Lord Milner, and that he was prepared to consider the question of transfer to which it referred. On the return of the two Ministers to the Union, however, the matter was again allowed to drop.

That no reply was given to the letter which had forwarded this memorandum to Lord Milner, is no doubt due to the fact that General Botha, who was ill when he left England, died at Pretoria in August 1919. His companion, General Smuts, was left to face a period of unusual economic strain and rising party animosities in the Union. There the question of the constitutional position of the Union within the Empire shortly became a contentious party issue. The question of the transfer of the Territories to the Union in turn acquired a new significance, in so far as the difficulty experienced in securing their incorporation in the Union came to be quoted as typical of the kind of treatment which might be accorded to a dependency which, while it might in most respects seem to enjoy a full measure of self-rule, had so far been denied the recognition of complete sovereign status. In June 1924 General Hertzog succeeded General Smuts as Prime Minister. He had throughout his political career in the Free State remained a firm adherent of the gospel of secession, and he now became the leading figure in the growing demand for the recognition of a status of full sovereignty for the Union. Holding strong opinions also on the need for fostering a 'White South Africa', for which a policy of segregation was in his view an essential instrument, he was in 1924 preparing four measures dealing with Native policy, one of which was the Native Land Bill. Among other objects, this was designed to fulfil the undertaking made in 1913 to provide more land for the Bantu, as one of the necessary conditions of the policy of segregation. The head committee of the Nationalist Party in the Transvaal had contended[9] that it was almost impossible to acquire the area needed for this purpose, unless more land could be secured by the incorporation of the three High Commission Territories in the Union. There can be no doubt that this consideration largely influenced the approach which the Prime Minister was to make to the High Commissioner (Lord Athlone) in October 1924, as also the statements on the subject of transfer which he was to issue to the Press in December 1924 and February 1925, and a speech he made in the House of Assembly in March 1925.[10] He asked the High Commissioner to ascertain the feeling of His Majesty's Government in the matter of incorporating all three Territories in the Union, a step which he felt to be essential to their development through railways and irrigation. He added that he had received petitions from the inhabitants of the Territories, in which they asked for incorporation. From the statement issued to the Press in December 1924 it appears that a deputation from Bechuanaland had asked him in that month to arrange for the incorporation of the Protectorate in the Union; the statement issued to the Press in February 1925 shows that a deputation from Swaziland had made the same request; but it also made clear that both deputations had come from the European inhabitants of the two Territories. The speech made by the Prime Minister in the House of Assembly gave the same information. He emphasized, however, that while he had told the deputations that in his own view the time was approaching to consider the incorporation of Bechuanaland and Swaziland, and that he would be prepared, if circumstances were favourable, to consider this, he had immediately added 'that we are not prepared to incorporate in the Union any territory unless the inhabitants of the territory are prepared to come in'. He now repeated this very significant declaration, in much the same words, to the

---

[9] Walker, op. cit., p. 620.   [10] Cmd. 8707, pp. 15–18.

members of the Assembly, adding that in referring to the
people of the Territories, he had included Natives as well as
Europeans.

General Hertzog received the answer to the communication
made to the High Commissioner in a detailed dispatch from
the Secretary of State for the Dominions dated 4 December
1925. Mr. Amery confined his answer to the definite issue which
had been raised in General Botha's letter of 1913, namely, the
transfer of Swaziland. He indicated that he did not consider
that the present time, when the Native policy of the Union was
about to be subjected to radical revision (an allusion to the
four Native Bills to which reference has just been made) was
one which was opportune for putting forward a proposal for
this measure. If General Hertzog proposed to ask for the transfer of administration in the following year, the British Government would be prepared to discuss the matter with him on that
basis. The inhabitants would of course have to be consulted,
and great prudence would have to be observed in choosing the
moment for such consultation, because if the reception were
such as to make it desirable to withdraw the application, it
would not be possible to renew the question for some years
to come.

Mr. Amery added that he understood that although the
Swaziland Advisory Council[11] had asked that the Territory
should be taken out of the Schedule of the South Africa Act,
they would be reconciled to the form of administration prescribed by it if Swaziland were granted representation as an
electoral entity in the Union Parliament. He expressed a
doubt, however, whether General Hertzog could hope to
secure the concurrence of the White population unless an
undertaking were given that the construction of a railway
through Swaziland would be commenced immediately on the
transfer being effected. But the chief concern of the British
Government, he added, was for the position of the Natives,
rather than that of the White population, and judging by

[11] That is, the European Advisory Council; see *Native Administration*,
Pt. V, pp. 377–8.

their attitude hitherto, they might not be inclined to regard with favour a proposal for transfer. It would be necessary to ascertain from General Hertzog how far the system of administration to which the Natives had been accustomed would be changed in the case of transfer, and how far the new Native legislation now proposed in the Union would affect the position of the Swazi. The question of land rights was especially important. The Natives would want to know whether the Native areas would be kept entirely for Native use. It seemed that thirty-five areas of Swaziland had been formally proclaimed as Native areas. Would the existing practice be maintained under which no persons other than Natives of Swaziland were allowed to reside in these areas without the permission of the Administration? There were similar questions to be answered regarding the membership of the Commission which was to be established under the Schedule to the Act of 1909, the provision to be made for the administration of justice, and the appointment of administrative personnel. It was emphasized that in suggesting that both the European and Native communities of Swaziland would require assurance on the points above mentioned, the Secretary of State was reflecting the experience of views which had been put by the Swazi to the officers of the local Administration in the course of numerous meetings at which the question of transfer had been discussed.

Mr. Amery's dispatch of December 1925 seemed to indicate that the British Government was now reaching a new stage in that progressive change of attitude regarding the question of transfer to which attention has been called in a previous part of this narrative. But it had not apparently arrived at a definite decision as to the answer which should be given to approaches made by the Union for the transfer to it of the Territories. In 1909 it had made no secret of its intention to hand over their administration to the Union; it was in fact only a question of time when this was to take place. It now had to face the fact that the outlook on Native policy held by the majority party in the Union was not at all that to which it had looked forward in 1909. In 1909 it had shown that it would only cede the Territories to the Union if its Government agreed to abide by the conditions laid down in the Schedule to the Act; it now seemed to doubt whether it could rely on the Union to abide by the spirit of these conditions in view of increasing proofs of the hardening of majority opinion in the Union regarding the treatment to be given to the Native people. On the other hand, the Union had stood by Great Britain during the war, and in doing so its Government had encountered grave risks of open division among its own European population. Great Britain could not now afford to give a flat refusal to General Hertzog's proposals for the transfer of the Territories, and prudence seemed to suggest the wisdom of compromising with the request he had put forward. He had for the moment concentrated on the question of the transfer of Swaziland, and it seemed possible that if Great Britain gave way in that matter, she might at all events secure a considerable period of delay before being forced to face a demand for the transfer of the other two Territories.

If one Territory was, so to speak, to be jettisoned, in order to safeguard the others, then there could be little question that it should be Swaziland. That Territory contained far the largest number of Europeans in proportion to Africans in its population. Though the area of lavish land concessions to Europeans made by Mbandzeni had been appreciably reduced by a Land Commission in 1907, the area remaining in Swazi hands was in 1925 still only about 49 per cent. of the total land area of the Territory.[12] Again, though respect for the Paramount Chiefdom is a very real fact in the religion of the Swazi, the actual organization of Native authority was in other respects weaker than in the other two Territories, and might therefore be the more easily replaced by institutions of the type favoured by the Union. The Secretary of State no doubt recalled also that Lord Crewe, speaking in the House of Lords on 3 August 1909, had said that it was probable that a request would be

---

[12] *Native Administration*, Pt. V, pp. 414–15.

made for the transfer of Swaziland within ten years, and had added that he could not say that such a request could be refused.[13]

It is not clear how far any of these considerations were present also in the mind of General Hertzog when he replied to the Secretary of State in his letter of 6 April 1926,[14] but he now studiously confined himself to discussion of the transfer of Swaziland, avoiding as far as possible more controversial issues. He agreed that it would be more opportune to defer any public discussion on this matter till the following year, so that his proposal should now be viewed as a request that transfer should take place in 1927 or early in 1928. He outlined his proposals for the parliamentary representation of the European inhabitants after transfer and expressed his conviction that a railway would be constructed in Swaziland at an early date after transfer. He could undertake that the provisions of the Schedule of the Act would be held to be fully applicable to the Africans in the Native Reserves (viz. the thirty-five areas as defined in the Proclamation of 1917), but some change in the Schedule procedure might have to be faced in regard to Swazi living outside the Reserves. The same might be the case in regard to the provisions of the Schedule regulating the con-stitution of the personnel of the Statutory Commission for which it made provision. He added further details regarding the application to Swaziland of Union regulations about customs, excise, the fixing of local rates, and the like, about which, however, he himself foresaw no difficulty.

This letter was transmitted as usual through the High Commissioner, and Lord Athlone wrote at once to General Hertzog promising to let him have his own comments on the proposals it contained. He now did so at considerable length in a letter dated 14 July 1926. He welcomed the suggestion that proposals for the transfer of Swaziland should be deferred until the latter part of 1927 or early 1928, by which time the Union Parliament would presumably have dealt with the four Native Bills put forward by General Hertzog. He did not question the

[13] Thompson, op. cit., p. 423.   [14] Cmd. 8707, p. 23 ff.

propriety of the approach now made for the transfer of Swaziland, and he confined himself to a technical examination of the degree to which General Hertzog's proposals complied with the safeguards for the Native inhabitants provided in the Schedule of the Act of 1909. The Secretary of State had, he said, warned his predecessor in 1913 that it was unlikely that Parliament would be willing to make any alteration in the terms of the Schedule. Moreover, the Duke of Devonshire, when he met the Swazi Chiefs in 1923,[15] had given their Paramount Chief an explicit undertaking that 'His Majesty's Government would not support in the House of Commons or elsewhere any proposal for transfer, if it involved the impairment of such native rights and interests' as were provided in the Schedule of the Act. Lord Athlone found it disturbing, therefore, that though General Hertzog did not suggest any alteration in the Schedule as regards Native rights, he would limit its application to the Swazi living in the Native Reserves. The Swazi people, he added, had shown themselves to be very jealous and vigilant in guarding their rights, and they would certainly accuse the British Government of bad faith if it proposed to curtail in this way the range of the safeguards provided for their protection.

There would [Lord Athlone argued] be nothing to prevent the Government in power in the Union from applying over at least two-thirds of the Territory the provisions of a measure like the Colour Bar Act or restrictions on the acquisition of land by individual Natives outside the Native Reserves might be imposed, e.g., on the lines of Section 1 of the Natives Land Act, 1913, without the Commission being afforded an opportunity of expressing its views.

There were some other points in which it was clear that the scheduled provision for the protection of Native interests might prove inoperative after transfer, should the Union Government of the day differ from the view taken by the British Government regarding its obligations to the Native inhabitants of the Territories. Without going into further detail, it is

[15] Cmd. 8707, p. 125.

sufficient to say that Mr. Amery now appears to have been convinced that it might prove hazardous to place before Parliament proposals in the form of those made by General Hertzog. He seems in fact to have concluded that the only real guarantee that could satisfy Parliament would consist of evidence, based on an experience extending over a series of years, that the transfer would not involve serious disabilities for the Native inhabitants of the Territories. If proposals for transfer were put before Parliament without the assurance afforded by this experience, it might involve a setback for a good many years, and give rise to much ill feeling.

This impression had, it seems, been strengthened by a recent visit which Mr. Amery had himself paid to the Territories, in the course of which he had received at first hand the evidence that the feeling against transfer was, if anything, more acute than at any previous time. He put these considerations before General Hertzog in the course of a discussion held in London during the autumn of 1927. He pointed out that the House of Commons, if it could be persuaded to accept proposals for transfer at all (which he regarded as out of the question as things then stood) would not only insist on close compliance with the conditions laid down in the Schedule, but might also demand a written pledge that the Schedule would remain intact for a long period of years after the transfers had taken place. He added that even the European inhabitants, who had once favoured transfer, seemed to have changed their position. Lord Athlone's letter of July 1926 had shown that they did not like General Hertzog's proposal that the Territory should after transfer be incorporated in the Transvaal Province, and Mr. Amery had now gathered that they had no desire for a transfer at the present time if the British Government could secure them a reasonable measure of development.

A note of these discussions was given to General Hertzog in a letter dated 6 September 1927, and a letter from the General received by Mr. Amery in the following month said that the note correctly summed up their conversation, though this did not imply that he accepted Mr. Amery's arguments regarding the advisability of awaiting the results of the working of what had been described as the 'new Native policy' embodied in his four Native Policy Bills. Nevertheless, General Hertzog made no move to re-open the question until 1932, when he addressed a letter, dated 30 November, to Mr. J. H. Thomas, then the Secretary of State for Dominion Affairs. In this he did little more than express his desire to re-open proposals for the transfer of the Territories to the Union. He did not give any definite reason for this desire, other than the fact that a question had arisen as to the need for 'reserving as much as possible fields of labour within the Union for the Union natives, with the consequential exclusion of natives from outside the Union'. Even to Mr. Thomas, a newcomer to the problems of Africa, it must have seemed somewhat unrealistic to suggest this reason for now re-opening the proposals for transfer, since as late as 1930 an Inter-departmental Committee on Labour Resources had emphasized that, except for a short period in 1924, there had not for many years been an adequate supply of labour in the country. Mr. Thomas does not seem to have replied to this letter, no doubt because General Hertzog was about to visit him in London.

From this point it is not easy to follow the course of the correspondence, partly because discussion was carried on through personal interview, and partly also because proposals for the incorporation of the Territories seem now to have arrived from a double source. In the summer of 1933 Mr. Thomas was having discussions with General Smuts, and on 21 July he handed to the General a Memorandum,[16] which has the appearance of a note prepared in order to provide him with a complete list of the pledges given by the British Government to safeguard the inhabitants of the Territories in the event of their transfer to the Union. On 28 July Mr. Thomas received from General Smuts a Memorandum prepared by Mr. Havenga, the Union Minister of Finance, who made, however, no reference to the approaches on the subject of the transfer of Swaziland which had been made by General Hertzog. On the

[16] Cmd. 8707, pp. 54–55.

other hand, much unnecessary effort was wasted by Mr. Havenga in demonstrating that the British Government had clearly intended in 1909 that the three Territories should be incorporated in the Union; he added indeed that the British had anticipated that the transfer would take place 'within a comparatively short period'. If there could be said to be any new argument of substance in his Memorandum, it took the form of an assertion that the Union had now to bear 'the brunt of the economic maintenance of the Territories', in so far that their products competed with those of the Union, though they were brought to the Union by Union railways and motor transport. It was added that the indigenous labour coming in from the Territories ousted Union labour, with the result that unemployed indigenous labour had to receive Union State assistance. There was, in all honesty, very little force in these arguments, as Mr. Havenga must have known. If they merit any place in a record of the discussions on the subject of transfer, it is only because they were a tacit admission that the Union now felt it needed some substantive reason for urging the case for transfer, other than the natural sense of disappointment that the British Government had so far delayed carrying out its avowed intention of handing over the Territories to its administration. Mr. Havenga omitted, however, to pay sufficient regard to the fact that what the British Government had held forth in 1909 was a settlement on conditions clearly stated at the time. These conditions had then been accepted as reasonable by the four Legislatures which now combined to make up the Legislature of the Union. Nevertheless, the only concrete proposal so far made by a Union Minister for the transfer of one Territory (Swaziland) had involved in one point at least a noticeable departure from these conditions.

Mr. Thomas was prompt in his answer to General Smuts. In a letter of 4 August 1933 he remarked that the General's Memorandum prepared by Mr. Havenga had omitted to observe the importance of the pledges given to the Native inhabitants which were detailed in his own Memorandum forwarded on 21 July 1933. He now took the opportunity of reinforcing the latter statement by enclosing an extract from certain debates in the British Parliament on 26 and 27 July 1933. The main point made in the course of these debates by the non-official speakers concerned was the importance of supporting the Natives in their opposition to transfer, while the Government for its part had reasserted its determination to bear fully in mind the pledges which they and preceding Governments had given to safeguard the position of the Natives if any proposal for transfer came forward. Mr. Thomas did not go on to discuss the 'administrative and economic advantage of transfer' on which Mr. Havenga had relied in putting forward his case.

There occurred at this point an incident which aroused for a time a good deal of public attention in the Union to affairs in Bechuanaland and which required an intervention by the Dominions Secretary and Prime Minister of Great Britain in the administration of the Protectorate. Tshekedi Khama, the Regent Chief of the Bamangwato tribe, had as president of its Tribal Court been responsible for carrying out the flogging of an Afrikaner youth; there was no doubt of the youth's guilt, nor that the type of punishment was appropriate to the offence; but the trial of a European was contrary to the local law, and the actual infliction of flogging was strongly resented by White opinion in the Union. Even so, the major attention of its public was perhaps engaged by the ridicule attaching to the almost comic-opera procedure adopted by the Admiral at Cape Town (acting temporarily as High Commissioner) for effecting the temporary removal of Tshekedi Khama from his position as Chief and his banishment from the tribal area. The ridicule was not unmerited; but serious discredit was incurred by the ineptitude of the department of the British Government which had left a very gallant naval officer to deal with a problem which neither his training nor his experience had equipped him to solve. The incident did not however seriously break in on the course of correspondence between the Dominions Secretary and Pretoria. Mr. Thomas had hardly dispatched the reply of August 1933 above related when he received a letter dated 1 October 1933 from General Hertzog, now back in Pretoria. In this letter the Prime Minister of the Union overlooked the fact that the advances which he had made in 1926 had been limited to proposals for the transfer of Swaziland, for he now took up the question of the transfer of all three Territories at the point where General Smuts and Mr. Havenga had left it earlier in 1933. The question, he said, had now an added importance for the public of the Union as, in addition to the economic considerations to which he had referred in 1926, there had been added 'the question of stock disease'.[17] He now pressed for a definite decision from the British Cabinet. He had the answer in a letter from the Dominions Office dated 27 November 1933. This, after referring once again to the many pledges which had been given both to Parliament and to the inhabitants of the Territories, stated shortly that the Cabinet did not feel that the present time was suitable for raising the question of the transfer of the Territories to the Union.

Undeterred by this somewhat peremptory rebuff, General Hertzog returned to the question in a letter dated 25 April 1934. He suggested that further delay in making a settlement favourable to the Union might create an unfavourable state of feeling in his country, which, he now said, was becoming more and more insistent. He feared, moreover, that with further delay the relationship with the Territories might become less friendly, to the detriment of all concerned. But when he sought to reinforce then such substantive arguments as he had used in 1926, which were based on the economic, administrative, and judicial aspects of the existing relationship, he failed to be any more convincing. He added a reference to the recent invasions of swarms of locusts as being typical of the dangers incurred by Union farmers, for these invasions, he said, would either not have occurred, or would have been successfully combated at an early stage, if the Territories had been under Union administration. East Coast fever and scab had added to

[17] Cmd. 8707, pp. 44, 45.

the difficulty of dealing with foot-and-mouth disease, to which
reference had been made in his previous letter. In the judicial
field difficulties had been experienced because witnesses from
the Union were required to appear before Protectorate Courts
in sparsely populated districts, with no facilities for travel. As a
final point, he reiterated part of the argument used by Mr.
Havenga regarding the influx of labour from the Territories,
which was, he said, ousting Union workers from employment,
a matter which would be easier to control, if the Territories
were an integral part of the Union. He urged that the Cabinet
decision communicated to him in the letter of 27 November
1933 should now be reconsidered, 'leaving it to the Union to
give such safeguards in respect of the matters which may cause
concern to you as will be conducive to a satisfactory conclusion
of the question'.

Those who intend to cite arguments of a technical character
in order to support their case in a political controversy need
to make certain of their facts before stepping into the arena,
for failure in this respect may gravely weaken their approach to
their main objective. General Hertzog had unfortunately
neglected this precaution. As pointed out in the reply now
sent by Mr. Thomas on 16 July 1934, the General, in laying
such stress on the ravages of locusts, had confused the invasion
due to the Desert Locust with that which had actually been
due to the invasion of a different type, the Red (or Brown)
Locust.[18] Moreover, in the campaign conducted against the
latter type of invader, the Union authorities had by agreement
taken charge of the operations in the Bechuanaland Protectorate, and had expressed themselves as fully satisfied with the
co-operation they had received. It was not difficult to give an
equally effective answer in respect of veterinary action taken
in the Territories to deal with foot-and-mouth and similar
diseases. The difficulties which had arisen in the field of judicial procedure had actually been adjusted, to the apparent
satisfaction of the Union authorities, twelve months before the

---

[18] For the locust invasions see *An African Survey*, p. 897 ff.

receipt of General Hertzog's letter. The report of the Inter-departmental Committee on the Labour Resources of the Union in 1930 appeared to give a convincing answer to the suggestion that indigenous Union labour actually suffered from the competition of 'migrant' labour from the Territories; the body of labour coming to the Union from this source was in any case much less than that recruited from other external territories under arrangements which had been directly negotiated by the Union Government, such as that made for securing labour from Mozambique.

Every Government has in its employment services whose duty it is to provide Ministers with the ammunition without which many would prove to be ineffectual either in attack or defence. On the present occasion Mr. Thomas could certainly congratulate himself that he had been better served than General Hertzog. But the major issue, so far from having been decided, had not even been debated. There emerges, however, one point of more than passing interest in this correspondence. The concluding words of the General's letter, quoted above, throw an interesting light on the position that he was now taking in furtherance of a policy of which he had become one of the outstanding champions. The British had taken their stand on the provisions of the Schedule to the Act of Union. But the Union was clearly no longer to be treated as bound by the limitations which it had been compelled to accept in 1909. General Hertzog had himself taken a leading part in the deliberations of the Imperial Conference of 1926[19] which had provided that definition of the autonomous status of the Dominions which was to be reproduced in the Statute of Westminster of 1931, and was shortly to be emphasized in the Status of Union Act and Union Seals Act of 1934.[20] The British might see in the recognition of that status little more than the legislative endorsement of a constitutional situation already well established in practice. But General Hertzog and his Afrikaner associates were proclaiming it as a hard-won victory

[19] Cmd. 2768, 1926.
[20] *An African Survey*, p. 153; also Walker, op. cit., pp. 636, 673.

for those who had sought to compel Britain to endorse the
higher position in the international world now achieved by the
Union. It is clear that General Hertzog hoped that in this
issue, also, persistence could wear down the British to the point
at which they would agree to transfer the Territories to the
Union, if not on its own terms, then at least on terms more
favourable to it than those dictated by the Schedule to the
Act of 1909.

One may be excused for wondering at this stage how far the
issue regarding the incorporation of the Territories had actually
become a matter of real moment for the general public of the
Union or of definite concern to the people of Great Britain. In
South Africa, any differences on political or economic issues
readily find expression in a great variety of ways, but there
seems in fact to have been at this stage little public pressure
for the transfer of the Territories. It is at all events noticeable
that the most earnest of the approaches to the British Government usually emanated from leaders who were accustomed to
receive their most active support from the Transvaal or the
Free State; it had clearly become a matter which was of
particular interest to the Afrikaner section represented in
Union politics. In Great Britain the subject seems to have
attracted little public attention till about 1933. That it came
prominently to the public notice in that year was due to a
combination of circumstances. In the first place Sir A. Pim's
Report on financial and other conditions in Swaziland had
been published in 1932, followed by that on the Bechuanaland
Protectorate in 1933. Some reference will subsequently be
made to the value of these two Reports, and of that on Basutoland (which was to be published in 1935),[21] in their revelation
of the extent to which the British Government had hitherto
neglected to show any definite concern for the economic and
social development of the three Territories. It was largely as a
result of their publication that the possibility of transfer of the
Territories to the Union was given prominence in a series of

[21] Cmd. 4114 (Swaziland); Cmd. 4308 (Bechuanaland); Cmd. 4907
(Basutoland).

articles in *The Times* by Miss M. Perham and Mr. Lionel Curtis. These subsequently formed the basis of their book *The Protectorates of South Africa*, which also attracted much public notice.[22] This was partly no doubt because the matter was presented in the form of a controversy between the two authors, Miss Perham urging strongly the advisability of further delay in considering transfer, Mr. Curtis urging the prompt acceptance of proposals for their incorporation. This was not because he was himself in favour of the Native policy of the Union, for that was far from the case. He had, however, taken an active part in the promotion of the Closer Union Societies of 1907 and 1908,[23] and he now foresaw in the differences arising from the question of incorporation of the Territories a possible source of cleavage in a field in which he held that the preservation of the spirit of unity must be regarded as the major consideration. He urged as an additional argument the fact that Great Britain had shown complete apathy in regard to the development of the economic and social standards of the people of the Territories.

It seems to have been partly as the result of the interest aroused by this book that a number of those concerned with the problems of South Africa and its people joined with Lord Lugard, Lord Lothian, and Lord Selborne in a deputation to Mr. Thomas, then the Secretary of State for the Dominions, in November 1934. It has been stated that the position occupied by the Union appeared to be so strong that the deputation felt the need of compromise, and suggested that instead of a simple refusal of incorporation, the Union should be offered a transfer by well-timed stages, together with a change in the current system of administration which would ensure that when the final stage arrived, the actual change would be almost imperceptible to the people of the Protectorates. It is not clear how far the case as set out by the deputation appealed to the

[22] The articles were published in *The Times* as follows: M. Perham, 28 September 1933, 5 and 6 July 1934; L. Curtis, 13, 14, and 15 May 1935; editorial article 15 May 1935.

[23] See above, p. 29, and Thompson, op. cit., p. 61 ff.

Secretary of State, but there were other public men, such as Sir Herbert Stanley, former High Commissioner for South Africa, who early in 1935 wrote to Lord Selborne deprecating the idea that the Natives of the Territories should 'have to pay the price for the maintenance of cordial relations between the United Kingdom and the Union'.[24]

However this may be, it seems clear that some part at least of the case put to Mr. Thomas had already occurred to him. He was wondering whether it might not be profitable to adopt a line of approach to the Union Ministers which differed in some respects from that followed by his predecessors. The Reports made by Sir Alan Pim had revealed to the British Government the need for definite measures of both administrative reform and economic assistance to the Territories. If the Union could now be associated in some of these measures, might not that form of co-operation bear fruit in mitigating the distrust which the Natives of the Territories felt against the prospect of transfer to the Union? He had in 1932 formed the acquaintance of some of the Union Ministers at the Ottawa Conference, and he now made in the course of his letter of 16 July 1934 something of a personal appeal for their 'co-operation and association' in the development of the Territories. The answer was given to Mr. Thomas by General Hertzog in person. The result was the issue of the Aide-Mémoire of 15 May 1935, representing their joint agreement, which was subsequently communicated to Parliament in the form of a White Paper.[25] This concluded with the words

we realize, of course, that some measure of co-operation already exists, but we feel that there are many directions in which it could be fruitfully extended. In particular it appears to us to be an essential condition of the success of such a policy that the native population should feel that the Union Government are working in concert with the local Administrations with a real and generous desire to develop and improve conditions in the Territories.

[24] M. Benson, *Tshekedi Khama* (Faber, 1960), p. 119; M. Perham, *Lugard* (Collins, 1960), Vol. II, p. 693.
[25] Cmd. 4948, 1935.

It is opportune to break off the narrative at this point in order to mention an interesting interlude in the discussions which were now taking place between General Hertzog and the Dominions Secretary. This took the form of a letter dated 27 March 1935 from the Governor of Southern Rhodesia, which in effect intimated that the Government of that Colony was prepared to undertake the administration of the Bechuanaland Protectorate rather than allow it to be handed over to the Union. It is the more appropriate to mention the matter here because the Aide-Mémoire had stated, when speaking of the pledges given to the inhabitants of the Territories by Great Britain in 1909, that the guarantees embodied in Section 151 of the Act of 1909 had not been affected by anything which had since occurred 'except insofar as the establishment of Southern Rhodesia as a self-governing Colony has a bearing on the future of at any rate part of the Bechuanaland Protectorate'. The purpose of this sentence was, it may be assumed, only to emphasize the fact that the precise terms of the Act, and in particular Section 150, might in any case need to be re-examined. It was not apparently intended to convey that the British Government felt that the interest shown by Southern Rhodesia in the future of Bechuanaland was of a nature which should seriously affect the course of negotiations actually in progress regarding the transfer of the Territories to the Union.

The move now made by Southern Rhodesia was not in fact entirely new, for in 1921 a Resolution[26] had been passed by the Legislative Council of the Colony (which was still at that time an appanage of the Chartered Company) that sought the incorporation into Southern Rhodesia of the area in the Bechuanaland Protectorate known as the Tati Territory. This Resolution had been put forward at the request of the European farmers resident in the Tati Concession (which forms part of the Protectorate), the case for the proposal being based both on general economic considerations and on the proximity of the Tati Territory to the Southern Rhodesian border.[27] The Colonial Office could in 1921 only reply that the terms

[26] Cmd. 8707, p. 127.   [27] *Native Administration*, Pt. V, p. 230 ff.

6

of the Resolution had been noted. But in 1923 the Colony
had acceded to the status of Responsible Government, nor
was its ambition now limited to the acquisition only of the Tati
Concession. It asked that the whole Protectorate should be
incorporated in Southern Rhodesia, 'or at least the northern
part of it'. It gave, as a specific reason for this proposal, 'the
apprehension felt in this Colony' lest the request by the Union
for the transfer to it of the administration of the High Commission Territories should be accepted. The 'northern' portion
of the Bechuanaland Protectorate was defined in the correspondence as an area which included the Francistown District,
together with an area of considerable size lying along the south
boundary of Southern Rhodesia and ending at the boundary of
South West Africa.

Mr. Thomas could only maintain a guarded attitude to the
request made in March 1935, and in his reply of 6 June 1935
was content to refer the Ministers in Southern Rhodesia to the
statement regarding co-operation with the Union which he
had just made in the House of Commons. Looking back now on
these proceedings, we may assume that the Southern Rhodesian
Government had regarded the Tati area at all events as especially suited for incorporation in their Colony. A large part of
it had been originally controlled by the Matabele, and it was
from Lobengula that the proprietors of the Tati Gold Mine
(which was by reputation the earliest goldfield worked by
Europeans in South Africa) had obtained their concession.
Though the gold diggings had since ceased to be remunerative,
a considerable area of land was still owned by the Tati
Company, and was for the most part leased to European
farmers or graziers. It is due to Southern Rhodesia to state,
however, that its Government now undertook that if this end
of the Protectorate was ceded to Southern Rhodesia it would
reconsider any local legislation which might seem to require
change in order to protect the interests of the Natives of the
areas thus transferred.

One can, on the other hand, appreciate the difficulty which
Mr. Thomas must have felt when he was invited to consider a

new commitment which might jeopardize the progress of that programme of co-operation with the Union to which he had for the time being pinned his hopes. On 21 May 1935 he wrote to the High Commissioner in South Africa requesting him to work out a method of co-operation between the Union Government and the Administrations of the Territories, 'the closer the better . . . over as wide a field as possible, and in particular in all matters relating to [their] economic welfare and development'. He told the House of Commons on 23 May 1935 that he believed this to be the best policy to pursue in the circumstances, 'so that if at any time a change takes place it will be with the good-will and co-operation of all parties instead of the hostility which would otherwise be there'. On 1 July 1935 the High Commissioner addressed to the Union Minister of Native Affairs an Aide-Mémoire containing suggestions for measures which might be followed in pursuit of the proposed policy of co-operation. Thus he suggested that the Territories should be given representation on the various local Boards set up by the Union for exercising control over the dairy, maize, meat, and tobacco industries. They would thus have a say in fixing the quota allowed for the export of cattle, or the railway charges for the transport of chilled meat. The Union, he added, might desire to be associated, financially or otherwise, in the schemes of development for which considerable sums of money were now (largely as the outcome of Sir A. Pim's Reports) being provided by the British Government, such as the drainage of the Okavango Delta in Bechuanaland, or the control of erosion in Basutoland. It might also desire to supply free of charge agricultural or other officers seconded to the Territories as advisers on water-boring schemes, pasturage development, and the like; and the Union Government might care to contribute to schemes of benefaction, particularly in the Native Reserves, such as those for hospitals, bridges, and possibly schools. Here, the High Commissioner believed, would be the best field for influencing Native opinion. While naturally prepared to give priority to supplementing the tardy assistance given by Great Britain to the

Territories, he declared himself to be equally anxious to do what was possible to influence the opinion of their Native inhabitants in favour of the Union.

The appeal for co-operation which Mr. Thomas had made to the Union Government in his letter of 16 July 1934, and had repeated in the discussions held in 1935, had not failed entirely of its effect. When the High Commissioner scheduled a number of schemes of development which were estimated to cost about £240,000 in the next four or five years, and suggested that the Union might make a contribution of £35,000 during the year 1936–7, General Hertzog agreed at once to accept this proposal. But when, however, this offer was communicated to the Native Authorities in the Territories by the three Resident Commissioners, accompanied by assurances that they would incur no liability by accepting Union money, it became clear that these assurances were not enough to dispel their fear of what might happen if their areas should eventually be incorporated in the Union.[28] So strong a feeling against acceptance of the contribution was in fact expressed by the Native Authorities, that the High Commissioner eventually found himself compelled to inform the Union Government that he could not hope for some time to ask that the contribution be actually paid. The offer was in consequence withdrawn by the Union Government.

Though General Hertzog had readily accepted the proposal that the Union should contribute to the cost of these schemes, it was unfortunate that he allowed himself an unwise latitude of expression when explaining his reasons for doing so in the Union House of Assembly on 16 June 1936. He began by saying that in his opinion it should not be necessary to wait for two or three years to elapse before Swaziland should be in the position of goodwill necessary to allow its transfer to the Union. He went on to add that the Aide-Mémoire of 1935 marked the first occasion since 1910 that the British representative 'had given an assurance' that the Territories 'would eventually be handed over'. He admitted to the Assembly that

[28] Walker, op. cit., p. 663.

no definite date had been mentioned; all that had been said (as he afterwards explained) was that they would be handed over in a few years and not at the same time but one after the other. Swaziland would probably be the first, Bechuanaland would follow, and thereafter Basutoland. He said that the £35,000 included in the Union Estimates was to help to secure the goodwill of the Natives for the hand-over. But if the Natives 'do not want to come in . . . [but] to hold themselves apart, then they must realise that the markets of the Union will no longer be open to them. . . . The longer they try to remain outside the more they will have to pay the penalty for it'.[29]

A competent observer has remarked[30] that General Hertzog was always inclined 'to take colour from his audience, to let his emotions run away with him, and to lose control over his words'. Here surely was a case in point. The discussions which had been held in 1935 are on official record. There is no mention in that record of the assurance said by General Hertzog to have been given by the British representatives regarding transfer, nor is there any mention of a time-table for the transfer. Reading General Hertzog's speech, moreover, one might infer that the British representatives had actually agreed to the transfer without observing any of the pledges given by the British Government regarding consultation with the Natives of the Territories. It is not astonishing, therefore, that the General should have received on 1 July 1936 a courteous but firm remonstrance from Mr. Malcolm Mac-Donald, who had succeeded as Secretary of State for the Dominions. It is to the General's credit that in reply he agreed that Mr. MacDonald should inform the House of Commons that his recent statements to the House of Assembly were only to be read 'as an expression of his personal hope that, if the policy agreed to in the Aide-Mémoire is loyally carried out by both Governments, a position would, within a few years, be created which would permit the transfer of the Territories to the Union with the goodwill of their populations'. An announcement was accordingly made to the House of Commons in

[29] Cmd. 8707, p. 65 ff.   [30] Hancock, op. cit., p. 243.

these terms on 16 July 1936. It may well be imagined, however, that the wide publication in South Africa of the news that
the British representatives had, without any prior consultation
with the Native Authorities, agreed to an early transfer of the
Territories to the Union, served to create an element of
distrust in them that seriously impaired the prospect of any
success in the programme of 'conciliation'.

It is regrettable, moreover, that General Hertzog, though
guilty of so serious a mis-statement in 1936, did not seem to
have appreciated the advisability of speaking in future by the
record. Thus on 6 July 1937, addressing a body of Press
representatives at Bloemfontein,[31] he asserted that in 1935 the
then British Minister concerned gave him, with the consent of
his colleagues, a written assurance, later made public, in which
the prospect was set out that transfer would possibly occur
after a year, at least so far as one or two of the Territories were
concerned. Moreover, he said,

I was told at the time that in order to expedite and assure transfer
as much as possible instructions would be given to British officials
entrusted with the administration of the Territory to use such
influence with the natives under their jurisdiction as would advance
the establishment of a disposition towards the Union that would
facilitate the achievement of the said purpose.

He now complained that no such instructions had been given,
and that it would consequently take a long time before transfer
would be possible. 'The Union's right to the transfer of the
administration of the Territories to it is indisputable. That the
time for transfer to the Union has already expired was
conceded two years ago.'

When Mr. MacDonald was asked in the House of Commons
on 10 July 1937 if the statement quoted above was correct,
he naturally recalled to the House that General Hertzog had
in the previous year (1936) concurred in his (Mr. MacDonald's)
informing the House of Commons that 'there was [in fact] no
agreement or understanding that the transfer of the Territories,
or any of them, should take place in any specified time'. As for

[31] Cmd. 8707, p. 70.

General Hertzog's assertion that no instruction had been issued to British officials in the Territories for implementing the policy of co-operation, there must, Mr. MacDonald added, have been some misunderstanding, for a copy of the instructions issued to the High Commissioner in connexion with the Agreement of 1935 had been shown to General Hertzog before they were sent, and he had concurred in their terms. Mr. MacDonald added, when speaking in the House of Commons on 28 July 1937, that he was prepared to produce to the House evidence that the instructions given in 1935 had been fully carried out by the administrative officers of the Territories. In a letter sent to General Hertzog on 25 September 1937, he detailed to him at considerable length the steps taken to ensure as far as possible that if and when a definite proposal for transfer came forward 'the native population should feel that the Union Government are working in concert with the local Administrations, with a real and generous desire to develop and improve conditions in the Territories'. He felt compelled in this letter to remark on the adverse effect on the Native population of certain statements made in the course of the debate in the Union Parliament in June 1936, which had led them to infer that the offer of aid from the Union Government had carried with it a condition regarding the transfer of some or all of the Territories within a set period of years. This had unfortunately led to a temporary breakdown of the policy of co-operation. He suggested, nevertheless, that certain measures might still be taken which would help to convince the Natives of the goodwill of the Union Government in this matter. One such measure would be the modification of restrictions on the export of cattle. Another might take the form of an explanation to be provided by the Union Authorities regarding the manner in which administration would actually be carried on in the Territories after transfer. Yet another move of some value would in his opinion, be to provide an explanation of the system of quotas, excise, etc., which would apply to the export of produce from the Territories to the Union.

One may well regret that Mr. Thomas and General Hertzog

had not been able to ascertain from each other the actual character of the co-operation which they had in mind when arriving at the Aide-Mémoire Agreement of 1935. If they had done so, both Mr. Malcolm MacDonald and the General might have been spared the interchanges on the subject which were afterwards to occupy so much of their time. General Hertzog replied to Mr. MacDonald in a long letter of 29 December 1937. He made it clear that his own view of 'co-operation' was much more dynamic than that which seemed to have been in the minds of Mr. Thomas and his successors at the Dominions Office. As he now explained, he had hoped to see officials in the Territories engaged in active discouragement of agitation against the Union, and in an effort 'to inculcate in the inhabitants ideas favourable towards transfer'. This, it seems, was the explanation of the complaint he had made of the failure of the British to carry out their side of the compact that he had made with Mr. Thomas. If any comment is now required on this interchange of amenities, it is only to express some surprise that Mr. Thomas should actually have hoped that the Natives of the Territories would abate their hostility to the Union merely because its Government had made a contribution to the cost of the development expenditure in the Territories. It was well known that the British Government had, as the result of Sir Alan Pim's Reports, agreed to provide the cost of an extensive anti-erosion scheme in Basutoland, of somewhat less extensive schemes for clearing the Okavango Waterways in Bechuanaland, and of the provision of surface dams in Swaziland. These were, it is true, a somewhat tardy recognition of its responsibilities for assistance to the High Commission Territories, and they formed in fact only a relatively minor part of the liberal assistance that was in subsequent years to be given to the Territories under the provisions of the Colonial Welfare and Development Acts of 1940 and the following years. There were among the Native Authorities in the Territories a growing number of men who were both intelligent and well-informed. They could appreciate that the sum which the Union was to provide would not in fact increase the benefits to be secured by the Territories, but would merely reduce the amount which was to be provided by the British Treasury.

There is one more comment that needs to be made. General Hertzog's attitude on the subject of transfer was now marked by increasing overtones of assurance and self-confidence. Mr. MacDonald's letter of 25 September 1937[32] had suggested that in view of the enactment of the Statute of Westminster in 1931 it might be wise to discuss whether some amendment might not be required in the section of the Schedule of the Act of 1909 which provided that any alteration in it could be reserved for the signification of His Majesty's pleasure. But when General Hertzog wrote on 29 December 1937 he would not admit that discussion on this point was now either necessary or appropriate, nor indeed any discussion as to the form of an alternative security for the population of the Territories on transfer. He asked Mr. MacDonald to realize that there had been a radical alteration in the position of 'the Government of His Majesty in the United Kingdom' and of 'the Government of His Majesty in the Union'. The former had consistently taken its stand on the provisions embodied in the Schedule to the Union Act of 1909. But under the provisions of the Status of Union Act of 1934 these provisions, if they could not be said to have disappeared, had become inoperative, since there was no provision now in force by which legislation enacted by the Union Parliament could be reserved for approval or disapproval of the Crown. If, therefore, His Majesty's Government in the Union of South Africa were willing to engage that in the event of transfer, the administration of the Territories should follow the lines laid down in the Schedule of the 1909 Act, that would only be because it considered that their administration should approximate to that already followed in the administration of the Transkei, a model which it desired to continue and extend.[33] But for the rest, speaking on behalf of His Majesty's Government in the Union, he desired to warn

[32] See p. 79 above.
[33] For the Transkei see *An African Survey*, pp. 421–2, 426–7.

His Majesty's Government in the United Kingdom that 'their policy and administration' of the Native peoples of South Africa 'must remain a matter of purely domestic concern'. It presented conditions such that it was 'difficult to understand how any efficient check or sound judgment could be exercised or formed by His Majesty's Government in the United Kingdom'. Apart therefore from the effect of the constitutional changes produced by the legislation above referred to, His Majesty's Government in the Union could not admit as practicable 'anything which carries the semblance of an admission that they are not completely competent to fulfil the trust which rests upon them'.

Coming to the practical proposals now made in Mr. MacDonald's recent letter, General Hertzog dismissed at once the suggestion that steps might be taken to relax any regulation relating to the entry of cattle to the Union, as this might arouse the hostility of White farmers, and his Government would only be prepared to face this, if it were placed in a position to use the argument that the relaxation of conditions was an exigency arising out of the transfer of the Territories. He would, however, take steps to provide the statements regarding quotas, excise, etc. which Mr. MacDonald had suggested. For his own part he would recommend the appointment of a Joint Advisory Committee to advise upon all necessary improvement schemes in the Territories. He did not now put this forward on the ground that such improvements might secure the goodwill of the Native inhabitants of the Territories towards transfer. He indicated in fact that propaganda for this purpose was now far less important than measures which might remedy the 'deplorable misunderstanding' in the United Kingdom itself regarding the Native policy of the Union Government. That policy sought, he said, to ensure a treatment of Natives 'which will at once be fair and just to them . . . and . . . compatible with the . . . preservation of European civilization in the Union and the whole of South Africa'. In this connexion he followed up his letter by one dated 16 February 1938, in which he reverted to a passage in the Aide-Mémoire of 1935, which had said that both Mr. Thomas and he himself thought that the policy of both Governments for the next few years should be directed to bring about a situation in which transfer 'could be effected with the full acquiescence of the population concerned'. He did not now approve of this wording. He did not think that it would be right to go beyond the pledge that had been given in 1909, namely, that transfer should not take place until the wishes of the Natives of the Territories had been carefully considered.

On 29 March 1938, Mr. MacDonald informed the House of Commons that he and General Hertzog had now agreed to establish a Joint Advisory Conference consisting of officers of the Union Government and the Resident Commissioners of the three Territories. It is of interest to speculate why General Hertzog had put forward the suggestion for the appointment of this Conference. We may assume that he thought that nothing was now likely to be gained if information regarding the good intentions of the Union Government were left to be conveyed to the Native Authorities by the British officials of the Territories. The Joint Advisory Conference would at all events bring on the scene a number of Union officials, who should provide a more favourable agency for this purpose. It was now to consist of the Union Government Secretaries for Finance, Native Affairs, and Agriculture, in addition to the three Resident Commissioners of the Territories.

The lines of General Hertzog's reminder of the change in the constitutional relations of the Union with the British Government may not have been entirely welcome to Mr. MacDonald, but there can be no question that his statement regarding this change was technically correct. It is a matter of some astonishment indeed that the Dominions Office does not seem to have shown before this time any active appreciation of the full extent of this change. The implications of the terms of the Statute of Westminster of 1931 had already caused it some concern in 1933, and at its suggestion the constitutional question had then been studied by a Parliamentary Committee under the chairmanship of Lord Selborne. In its Report dated

31 July 1934[34] the Committee felt no difficulty in stating that the enactment of the Statute of Westminster in 1931 and of the South African Status Act of 1934 had the result of repealing all those sections of the South Africa Act of 1909 which made provision for reservation of legislation to the King as advised by His Majesty's Government at Westminster. 'Henceforth the Parliament of the Union of South Africa may repeal or make any amendment it chooses of the Sections, and Articles of the Schedule, of the South Africa Act, 1909, and neither H.M.G. nor the Parliament at Westminster will have any constitutional status for expressing any opinion on the subject.' But at this point the Committee seems to have felt itself constrained to pass beyond the interpretation of the Statute, and it proceeded to point out that the Union was committed to implement certain basic principles for the future government of the Territories which 'were agreed between the South African Convention and the British Parliament and ratified by the Parliaments of the four South African Colonies'. Whether this would be accepted by constitutional lawyers as now creating a definite commitment of the Union Government is open to doubt, and it is therefore pertinent to study the terms of a Memorandum prepared by the Government of the Union and sent to the British Government in the course of 1939. This was the Memorandum the preparation of which had been forecast by Mr. MacDonald in his letter to General Hertzog of 29 December 1937, as explaining the terms on which the transfer of the Territories would take place if and when it might be approved.

The contents of the Memorandum were in some respects more reassuring than might at one time have seemed likely. The Prime Minister and Government of the Union now indicated that the system of administration after transfer would in fact correspond to that detailed in the Schedule to the Act of 1909; if any alteration in the terms of the Schedule should be contemplated by the Union Government, it would consult with the British Government and give due consideration

[34] Cmd. 8707, p. 131.

to any observations it might make. The powers and status of the Chiefs would continue unchanged, and in other respects the existing form of administration would be maintained. The British Government had thus obtained from the Government of the Union an undertaking that in the event of transfer it would observe in substance some of the safeguards for Native interests for which provision had been made in the Schedule to the Union Act. The Union now went on, moreover, to guarantee that the existing educational, medical, and other social services, together with the schemes for veld reclamation, the combating of soil erosion, and similar objects, would be maintained. A special clause was added to safeguard the provisions of the Swaziland Proclamation 2 of 1915, which made provision for controlling the purchase by Natives of land in Swaziland, and for securing for the benefit of the Swazi people any land marked as specifically acquired for the Swazi nation. In the world of international affairs general statements of principle seem to be susceptible of a great variety of interpretation in practice, and what matters to the Native populations which may be affected by them is less the announcement of the principles which they set forth than the chance of their application in practice. It is therefore of interest to note that General Hertzog had in his letter of 29 December 1937 specified that the administration of the Transkei Territories by the Union would provide a model to be followed in that of the High Commission Territories, if these were transferred to the Union. The system to which General Hertzog referred as followed in the Transkei was admittedly more liberal than that practised in some of the districts of the Ciskei[35] but it would be out of place to discuss now whether all its features would be acceptable for adoption in the High Commission Territories, since, as will subsequently be shown, there have in more recent years occurred dramatic changes in both the constitutional and the administrative policy of Government in the Transkei.[36]

Whether the proceedings of the Joint Advisory Council on

[35] *An African Survey*, pp. 422, 427–8.   [36] See p. 115 ff. below.

Co-operation fulfilled the purpose sought by General Hertzog himself is open to doubt; they certainly contributed little in any other respect. The first Report of the Council was issued in February 1939.[37] It had so far been able to deal only with Swaziland and part of Bechuanaland, and it was perhaps inevitable in consequence that it should devote most of its attention to the discussion of the possibilities of improvement in the production and marketing of cattle and the control of cattle disease, both of which were matters of primary importance in Bechuanaland. There was very little attempt to appraise the value of the many schemes of economic improvement which had since 1933 begun to receive assistance from the British Government.

The receipt of General Hertzog's letter of 29 December 1937 and of the Memorandum prepared by the Union Government in 1939 brought to an end the series of 'Discussions and Negotiations' between the two Governments of which publication was, by mutual consent, made in London in 1952 and in Pretoria during 1952–3. There was a break in formal exchanges during the period of the Second World War, though in 1943 General Smuts took occasion to express a hope that the Union might be allowed to take over the administration of the three Territories, if only as a reward for its war services.[38] In the course of the war the African people of the Territories provided a large body of volunteer labour, in the first instance for service in the Middle East, but subsequently also for service in North Africa, Italy, and Syria. They were originally enrolled as part of the 'African Pioneer Corps of the British Army', but under what became known as the process of dilution they actually took part in numerous duties of a combatant character, such as service in the anti-aircraft gun teams. Towards the end of the war a considerable number of men were enrolled in a newly-formed 'High Commission Territorial Corps'.[39]

Shortly after the conclusion of peace, the Government and Press of the Union found cause to complain of the action taken

[37] Cmd. 8707, p. 90.   [38] Walker, op. cit., p. 735.
[39] Sillery, op. cit., pp. 213–18.

by a number of Bechuanaland Chiefs, in addressing the newly-formed United Nations Organization on behalf of the section of Herero settled in the Western area of Bechuanaland. This settlement had its origin in an infiltration of Damara tribesmen from Namaqualand about the year 1891, but these had been reinforced in 1905 by a large party of Herero, headed by Frederick Maherero, who had sought asylum in Bechuanaland from the German 'War of Extinction' against the Herero of South West Africa.[40] When in 1945 the Natives of South West Africa were asked their views on suggestions that had been made for the incorporation of the Mandated Territory in the Union, the Herero, almost alone among the tribes concerned, had made a marked stand in opposition to the proposal, and had indicated a strong preference for the transfer of the Mandate to Great Britain. Five of the Bechuanaland Chiefs, headed by Tshekedi Khama, then Regent Chief of the Bamangwato tribe, had petitioned the United Nations Organization in their support. It was urged by the Union Government that their action was a gratuitous intervention in a matter in which they had no direct concern; but it was said in their defence that as Bechuanaland abutted for 500 miles on South West Africa, they feared that if that country were incorporated in the Union she might go on to incorporate Bechuanaland also.[41] Whatever the justification for this apprehension, it is clear that Union Ministers reacted strongly against the steps now taken by the Bechuana Chiefs concerned and by their missionary sympathizers, realizing that their real object was to reinforce the growing opposition shown in the United Nations Organization against the current Native policy of the Union. That was a matter which, as the Ministers could maintain with some justice, was one of domestic concern, and consequently beyond the legitimate purview of the United Nations.[42]

Towards the end of September 1948, another incident occurred (again having its origin in Bechuanaland) which had a much more direct impact on relations between the Territories

[40] *Native Administration*, Pt. V, pp. 182–3, 262 ff.
[41] Benson, op. cit., p. 153.   [42] *An African Survey*, pp. 173–4.

and the Union than the interest which had been shown by some of the Bechuana Chiefs in the cause of the Herero. Seretse Khama had been designated as Ruling Chief of the Bamangwato in succession to Sekgoma II, who had died in 1925. While still a student at Oxford he had announced his engagement to an English girl, and in spite of efforts made by the Regent Chief, his uncle Tshekedi Khama, and by some other leading members of his tribe, in order to secure delay of his marriage until the tribe had agreed to accept the position which would be created by it, he had insisted on its being performed at once at an English registry office. It appeared subsequently that the tribe felt in fact less opposition to the marriage than had been expected, but opinion in the Union reacted strongly to news of the marriage of an English woman to an African. The strength of this feeling was shown when in 1949 the Mixed Marriages Act passed by the Union Legislature declared null and void any marriage contracted between White and non-White persons, and when, in the following year, the Immorality Act signalized carnal intercourse between White and non-White persons as a serious offence under the criminal law. There can be little doubt that when the British Government decided to exclude Seretse from residence in Bechuanaland for five years, it was influenced by the feeling in the Union on the subject of his marriage.[43] It has been stated that Dr. Malan, who had succeeded as Prime Minister of the Union in June 1948, had conveyed to the British Government in unequivocal terms the views of the Union Government on the subject of the marriage, and that General Smuts, as Leader of the Opposition, had stressed to British Ministers the danger of recognizing Seretse as the Chief of his tribe, because 'White South Africans were hardly sane on the subject of miscegenation'. If, therefore, Seretse and Ruth his wife were to be installed, the Nationalist Government would surely demand the incorporation of Bechuanaland, and possibly even threaten to blockade the Territories. His own party, he is said to have

[43] Walker, op. cit., p. 803, and M. Perham, at p. 4 of the Introduction to Tshekedi Khama's pamphlet entitled *Bechuanaland* (1955).

added, 'would be unable to oppose such a move because of the emotions aroused'.[44] That the British Government of the day should in fact be so far influenced in this direction is perhaps the more noteworthy because the Labour Party had come into office in July 1945 and were still in power.

In 1949 Mr. Huggins, the Prime Minister of Southern Rhodesia, appears to have referred again to the claim originally made in 1935, that his country retained a right of succession to the administration of that part of the Bechuanaland Protectorate which Great Britain had engaged in 1895 to make over to the Chartered Company.[45] This brought into the field Dr. D. F. Malan, who claimed that any such co-partnership in the control of the Protectorate as Mr. Huggins had seemed to contemplate would conflict with the agreement made by the British and South African Governments in 1909, that the disposal of the High Commission Territories should be a matter exclusively for their respective Governments. As a matter of fact, any such claim made on behalf of Southern Rhodesia need have caused no greater disquiet to Dr. Malan than the speech made by Sir Starr Jameson should have caused to General Botha in 1913.[46] The legal personality which the Chartered Company had acquired from the British Crown as an agency of administration must surely have vanished when its Charter terminated in 1924. But it is possible that Dr. Malan, like General Botha, really saw in the claim made on behalf of Southern Rhodesia a suitable ground for renewing on behalf of the Union that demand for the incorporation of the three Territories which had occupied so much of his predecessor's activity between 1924 and 1938.

When he was in London for the Prime Ministers' Conference in 1949 Dr. Malan restated to the Secretary for Commonwealth Relations the Union Government's view on the subject of transfer. He referred to this interview when speaking in the

---

[44] Benson, op. cit., p. 200. Such letters as have been preserved in the Smuts Archives bear out part only of the version given in the text above.
[45] See p. 52 above.
[46] See p. 54 above.

7

following year in the Union House of Assembly (13 April 1950). He then said

. . . I then told them . . . that the people of South Africa were becoming impatient, because in spite of numerous attempts which had been made in the interim, almost 40 years had passed without anything having been done. . . . I pointed out that the British Government had not yet done anything, and that we had received only negative replies.[47]

He added that he had warned the British Minister that the South African Parliament would have to take the initiative, and he now suggested that a petition should be addressed to the British Parliament (rather than to the Privy Council as had been prescribed in Section 151 of the Union of South Africa Act) asking for the transfer of the three Territories.

In the month of February 1951 the British Secretary for Commonwealth Relations visited the three Territories and also Cape Town. There Dr. Malan again mentioned to him the question of transfer, and in the course of a subsequent speech to his party he repeated the points he had made on this occasion. One such point raised an issue of considerable importance.

Whether the delay is due to the fact that we are not trusted with the protection or promotion of Native interests you will best be able to judge. . . . But apart from the question of grievous mistrust there is another aspect of this outstanding question which as a member of the Commonwealth we cannot ignore. It affects our equal status and place among the other members of the Commonwealth as well as our self-respect as a nation. . . . Constitutionally [the Union] stands on a footing of equality with the other members of the Commonwealth. . . . But in one vital respect she differs from them all, and that is, that within her embrace, and even actually within her borders, she is compelled to harbour territories, entirely dependent on her economically, and largely also for their defence, but belonging to and governed by another country. Such a condition . . . will not for a

[47] N. Mansergh (ed.), *Documents and Speeches on British Commonwealth Affairs, 1931–1952* (O.U.P. for R.I.I.A., 1952), Vol. II, p. 922.

single moment be tolerated, in their case, either by Canada, or Australia or New Zealand, not to speak of India or Pakistan or Ceylon or Britain herself. And so long as this is tolerated . . . there can be no real equality, nor even full independence for her. . . .[48]

The Secretary for Commonwealth Relations had pointed out in reply that there was one aspect of the problem which the Prime Minister had not mentioned, namely, the views of the inhabitants of the Territories concerned. 'We feel that no people anywhere, whether we are responsible for them or not, should be moved from one jurisdiction to another without full consideration of their views on the matter.'

Dr. Malan returned to the question when speaking at the Orange Free State National Party Provincial Congress in September of 1951. He then said that the question of transfer would if necessary be made an issue at the next General Election of the Union. This suggestion gave point to a statement made by the British Prime Minister, Sir Winston Churchill, in the House of Commons on 22 November following, when he pointed out that the British Government felt itself bound by the pledges given by previous Governments that the transfer should not take place until the inhabitants of the Territories had been consulted and Parliament had had an opportunity of expressing its views. The subject of transfer did not in fact become an issue in the Union Election of 1953, though Dr. Malan had in the interval shown that he maintained the same attitude as in 1950 and 1951. Thus, speaking at the Transvaal National Party Congress in September 1952, he had said that if friendly negotiations did not succeed in securing the transfer, then the Union would have the right to demand customs payments from the three Territories, and the Protectorate Natives would become ineligible for South African social welfare benefits when resident in the Union. After his re-election, he said in August 1953 that he hoped that the question would be settled within the next five years (the term of office of the Nationalist Government) 'without any of the assurances

[48] *Mansergh*, op. cit., pp. 928–9.

which some were demanding that Africans should have a say in Southern African affairs'.[49]

Early in 1954 the Secretary of State for Commonwealth Relations discussed at great length with Dr. Malan the question of the transfer of the Territories to the Union, and a full account of their discussion was afterwards given to the Press.[50] It was possibly recollection of the arguments used by the Secretary of State on this occasion, and his reiteration of the pledges given by the British Government regarding consultation with the inhabitants of the Territories, which moved Dr. Malan to utilize the question of transfer as a topic which would help to rally public opinion in South Africa to show its interest in the Nationalist Party programme. On 7 April 1954 he gave notice that he would introduce in the House of Assembly a Resolution dealing with the subject. It subsequently appeared that he had private discussions with the leader of the United Party in order to avoid opposition from that party in the Assembly. In this, however, he seems to have failed, for when the motion was moved by him on 12 April it was made obvious that though the United Party was prepared to support the claim for transfer, it was determined to oppose the Prime Minister's motion on the ground that he was tactically wrong in the manner of his approach to the question. His motion had urged that the transfer of the Protectorates should take place as soon as possible and that immediate negotiations to this end should be resumed immediately at the point reached at the outbreak of war in 1939. It is difficult today to understand why the debate on this motion engendered a heat which again and again set the Assembly in uproar. There was no difference of substance between the two parties, for the Opposition failed to indicate a more profitable line of approach which would in its view secure the purpose at which the motion had pointed. The explanation perhaps lies in the fact that the real objective

---

[49] *Commonwealth Survey*, 26 August 1953, and Walker, op. cit., p. 853. See also L. van der Post, *Daily Telegraph*, 13 February 1953, and the *Johannesburg Star*, 28 December 1953.
[50] *Johannesburg Star*, 11 January 1954.

of the Prime Minister was to demonstrate the vitality of Nationalist policy; the objective of the Opposition was a general condemnation of this policy. If strong convictions were shown on the issue of transfer itself, it was rather on the part of Dr. Malan than on that of the Opposition. He took the opportunity of the debate to speak of the position of the Protectorates as an 'intolerable encroachment on the rights of South Africa'. Great Britain, he added, had yielded to local pressure everywhere else; she had given up India, Burma, Pakistan, Ceylon, and other territory in the East; it was only in the case of South Africa that she had refused to give way.

His Resolution was carried in the House of Assembly on 13 April, and on the following day in the Senate. On the same day as the vote was taken in the Assembly, Sir Winston Churchill answered a question on the subject in the British House of Commons. He reiterated that we were pledged not to transfer the Territories until the inhabitants had been consulted, and the British Parliament had had an opportunity of expressing its views. He went on to recall to the House General Hertzog's statement that his party 'was not prepared to incorporate in the Union any Territory unless its inhabitants wished it'. He hoped, therefore, that the Union Ministers would 'not needlessly press an issue on which we could not fall in with their views without failing in our trust'.[51] It would seem that Sir Winston Churchill's answer was badly received in Nationalist Party circles in South Africa, and one Nationalist paper proceeded to describe Basutoland as a 'breeding ground of Communism'. There were, it seems, some members of the party who actually urged the Prime Minister to seize all the Territories without delay.[52]

In the course of his various references to the subject of transfer Dr. Malan had made two points of some substance. He had complained that he could not organize his country's defence unless he had control of the Territories, and he had pointed out that there existed in Basutoland the headwaters of

[51] *Hansard*, House of Commons, 13 April 1954, Col. 966.
[52] Walker, op. cit., pp. 912, 913.

rivers the development of which for irrigation purposes might, if carried out by the Union, prove of the highest value to great stretches of its country.[53] The reference to the subject of defence was made in connexion with the discussions which had taken place for the preparation of a joint scheme of defence for Africa south of the Sahara, in the course of which International Conferences had been held at Cape Town and Dakar. There was, however, something much less substantial in the assertion he made on another occasion regarding the conduct of the British officials in the Territories. They were, he said, 'systematically stiffening the backs of their Africans against the transfer'. He produced, however, no evidence in support of this charge.

Dr. Malan was succeeded as Prime Minister in December 1954 by Mr. J. G. Strydom. Shortly after taking office he assured his party that he intended to assume Dr. Malan's moral obligation to secure the transfer of the High Commission Territories to the governance of the Union. In this respect there was clearly to be no change of Nationalist policy, but it is interesting to note that the party's newspaper *Dagbreek* suggested in August 1955 that the Union Government should abandon its policy of demanding transfer. It should now seek some form of co-operation with Britain, in order to develop the Territories as Native Reserves, thus forming part of the plan put forward in the Tomlinson Commission Report of 1955.[54] The Territories would thus form three of the seven Reserves for the Bantu people. Dr. Verwoerd, then Minister for Native Affairs, said in a debate in the Union House of Assembly in May 1956 that the inclusion of the Territories in the Union was not basically essential for the implementation of the policy of segregation, though it would be in the interests of the inhabitants of the Territories themselves. Nevertheless, when Mr. Strydom was in London during July 1956 for

[53] On this point see also p. 111 below.
[54] *Summary of the Report of the Commission for the Socio-Economic Development of the Bantu Areas* (Pretoria, 1956). The Report itself was issued as U.G. No. 61 (1955). On the point mentioned in the text see p. 115 ff.

the Prime Ministers' Conference, he reiterated the desire of the Union Government for the transfer. The House of Commons was, however, told that the British Government had restated its position on this occasion also, and that no agreement was reached.[55]

[55] *Hansard*, House of Commons, 10 July 1956, Vol. 556, Col. 195.

V

OPINION IN THE TERRITORIES
ON INCORPORATION

THE preceding narrative has had much to say regarding the
exchanges between the Governments of Great Britain and of
the Union regarding the transfer of the three Territories. But
it has said far less of the views held by the third party to the
controversy, the people of the Territories, though to them the
issue was actually more vital than to either of the two major
protagonists. To the Union Government indeed the issue seems
to have become in course of time largely a matter of prestige
rather than of substantive importance. Of later years, however, a new note seems to have crept into the urgency with
which some of the Union Prime Ministers have sought to
secure British assent to the transfer. As suggested by Dr. Malan,
they could now urge that the retention of the Territories by
Great Britain was a practical denial of that status of independent sovereignty for which the Union Ministers had contended,
and which had been conceded to it by the Statute of Westminster. This might well prove to be a more powerful argument
than the urge to defend the principle of *apartheid*, for there have
been in the Union many Europeans who, while they have
accepted the ideology of *apartheid*, have had serious doubts
about its implementation in practice. But they might be
willing to support Union Ministers in a protest against anything that might appear to challenge the sovereign status of
their country.

There has also been some change of front on the part of the
British Government. It has been shown above that, when the
Transvaal Government refused in 1906 to accord any political
rights to Natives, the British Government laid down that,
pending any grant of representation to Africans, no Native

territory administered by the Governor or High Commissioner would be placed under the control of the new Responsible Government.[1] It would accordingly have been reasonable to assume at that date that if the new Responsible Government in the Transvaal had been willing to extend the Cape franchise to its Natives, then Swaziland (and perhaps Basutoland) would have been handed over to it without further question of the views held by their inhabitants. It will be remembered that there had been no question of 'consultation' with the tribes concerned, still less of gaining their assent, when British Bechuanaland (originally part of the Protectorate) was incorporated in Cape Colony in 1895. When, however, the question of the unification of the four Colonies of South Africa was mooted in 1907–8, the Imperial Government had further thoughts on the subject, and insisted that terms should be laid down against 'the probably far distant day' of transfer of the three Territories, and it was in compliance with this requirement that the members of the National Convention joined in providing the material for the 'safeguards' which afterwards reappeared as the Schedule to the Act of Union. The machinery which this prescribed for safeguarding the administration of the Territories after transfer is elaborate; but nowhere either in the Act or in the Schedule was it laid down that the inhabitants of the Territories must be consulted on the question of transfer. It was left for the spokesmen of the Liberal Government of the day to assure the British Parliament that the inhabitants would be 'consulted', but it was also clearly indicated that their agreement was not to be essential. The Government nevertheless continued to allow it to be understood that it was their intention that the Territories would at some subsequent time be transferred to the administration of the Union, subject to the acceptance by the latter of the conditions for transfer embodied in the Schedule. When, however, there was evidence of a progressive hardening of the attitude of the Union Government on Native policy, the British Government was left in an invidious position. It had

[1] See p. 25 above.

become obvious that the British public now viewed with definite repugnance the idea of transferring the Territories to the administration of the Union, but successive constitutional changes had tended to give the Union the character of a sovereign state member of the Commonwealth, and its Native policy had assumed progressively the character of a domestic concern of a sovereign state. Nor ought one to overlook the fact that for much of this period the Union was for British Ministers a Commonwealth country which had, at the risk of internal troubles, taken an active part in the First World War. For them it was the country of Botha and of Smuts, and even if at a somewhat later stage General Hertzog stood out with great pertinacity for the recognition of the Union as an independent sovereign state, his personal relations with the British Cabinet continued to be friendly and co-operative. In the British fashion, the decision at which its Government had arrived had been the result of instinct rather than of reasoning. Its decision was right, but the halting manner of the approach made to it had created a serious difficulty in giving effect to its terms. The one decisive argument which the British could now have used was to declare that the opposition of the inhabitants of any of the three Territories would form an effective barrier to its transfer to the Union. But the Government was precluded from the use of this reply by the declarations it had itself made at an earlier date.

Though the share taken by the people of the Territories in this controversial issue had not been spectacular, there can be no doubt of the answer which would have been given by the majority of their inhabitants, had the question been put to them. The European section of the inhabitants, for which transfer to the Union might have had some attraction, is relatively small in number. In Basutoland they numbered at the census of 1956 a total of 1,926 out of a total population of 638,857, but only a small number of these were permanent residents, since it had been agreed between the local Administration and the Basuto Native Authorities that non-Natives admitted for any specific purpose, such as traders, officials, or missionaries, would not be allowed to continue to live there after they had ceased to have an active interest in the Territory.[2] There were in Bechuanaland, according to the census of 1956, only 3,173 Europeans out of an estimated total population of 300,000.[3] Reference has been made above to the interest shown by the Europeans (who live mainly in the eastern and north-eastern part of the Territory) in proposals for transfer to the Union, but this interest does not seem to have been either strong or of a permanent character. Europeans have a far more important position in Swaziland. They numbered in 1956 a total of 5,919 out of a total of 240,511, but they owned roughly 48·5 per cent. of the land area.[4] For special reasons, such as the prospect of securing railway facilities, some of the Europeans in Swaziland have been at certain times in favour of incorporation in the Union.[5]

There is no reason to doubt that the Native Authorities in all three Territories have maintained the feeling against incorporation to which, as shown above, they have at various stages of their history given expression. It may, however, be held that the time has passed when views expressed by the Native Authorities or tribal Chiefs on any crucial issue could be taken as decisive evidence of the wishes of the Native inhabitants of a Territory as a whole. Nor indeed have there been since the critical year 1909 many Chiefs who have commanded a position such as some of their predecessors held in the past. Moshesh, 'the founder of the Basuto Nation', had throughout been a strong advocate for what he himself described as 'direct rule by the Queen of England's own representatives', but he had no personal experience of the period when Basutoland was administered as part of Cape Colony, for he died a year before the Act of Annexation to the Cape was passed. He left no successor of comparable standing or personal character,

[2] *Annual Report, Basutoland, 1960*, p. 35.
[3] In 1961 a 'sample' counting taken in Bechuanaland suggested a total population of 316,578. Similar figures taken in Swaziland in 1961 gave a total of 8,040 Europeans and 270,000 Africans.
[4] *Native Administration*, Pt. V, p. 414.
[5] See pp. 57 and 58 above.

but it is perhaps worth quoting, as evidence of the sentiments held by the numerous class known as 'Sons of Moshesh', the petition which was sent to the King of England by the Queen Regent in 1953. She then asked him to send Englishmen to take the place of the numerous Union nationals in the Civil Services of the three Territories, who alarmed her people by coming from a country whose Government was set on proclaiming a republic, 'a thing which we Basuto detest'.[6] There has been more than one case in the modern history of the Territory in which strong feeling has been shown against administrative officers on the sole ground that they happen to have been born in the Union, though British by origin and upbringing.

In Bechuanaland Khama III, a figure of authority comparable with that of Moshesh, at all events in his tribe, the Bamangwato, lived until 1923, and had therefore in his declining years some considerable experience of relations with the Union Government. It is on record that up to his death he continued to insist that his allegiance was only to the British Government, and that he was strongly opposed to incorporation in the Union.[7] His successor, Sekgoma II (1923–5), gave a firm reply to the proposals made by the Union on the subject of incorporation. 'We are', he is reported to have said, 'a contented people, not like those . . . under the Union Government. . . . We strongly oppose any effort to include the Bamangwato reserve in the Union.'[8] The younger son of Khama III, Tshekedi Khama, who was for many years the Regent Chief of the Bamangwato and proved to be one of the most outstanding figures in the tribal areas of Africa, showed himself to be of the same opinion as Sekgoma. In a work published in 1955, he maintained that, in his own words, 'there are for the people of Bechuanaland no reasonable grounds to support the proposal that the Territory should be transferred to the Government of the Union of South Africa'. He said that in advocating the creation of a fully representative

[6] Walker, op. cit., p. 803.
[7] A. E. Blackburne, *Khama of the Bamangwato* (1926), p. 16.
[8] Benson, op. cit., p. 45.

Legislature for the Protectorate, he sought means whereby expression of this view could be given by a national organ of recognized authority.[9] But this was only one of the numerous ways in which he expressed his concern lest the British Government should yield to the attempts made by Union Ministers to secure the transfer of the Protectorate to the care of the Union. It is also significant that Seretse Khama, the recognized heir to the position of Ruling Chief of the tribe, was reported in the Press as having stated that any future for the Protectorate, even absorption in Southern Rhodesia, would be preferable to incorporation in the Union.[10]

In Swaziland the Paramount Chief Sobhuza II, soon after succeeding to full powers in 1921, was actively engaged in legal proceedings of much importance to the Swazi community, which terminated in an appeal to the Privy Council. These proceedings dealt specifically with the rights retained by the Swazi in the lands which had been the subject of the widespread concessions made by his predecessor, Mbandzeni, but the legal issues discussed involved also problems regarding the constitutional position of Swaziland. In 1940, 1944, and 1954 Sobhuza took part in a series of somewhat contentious discussions regarding draft Proclamations designed to define the status of the Swazi Native Authority. As had already been shown, he and his people have proved themselves to be very vigilant in protecting their rights, but nowhere in those proceedings was there any indication of a feeling that their position could be improved to their benefit by incorporation in the Union.

It may well be held, however, that Native Authorities in the Territories may have some personal feeling against the incorporation of their Territories in the Union, for though the result of the internal reforms introduced in 1934 in Bechuanaland, in 1939 in Basutoland, and in 1944 in Swaziland[11]

---

[9] Tshekedi Khama, op. cit. See also on this point *Native Administration*, Pt. V, pp. 334, 429.

[10] *Daily Express*, 28 February 1962.

[11] *Native Administration*, Pt. V, pp. 218 ff., 88 ff., and 385 ff.

were primarily directed to systematizing the powers of the traditional Native Authorities, they still left them a higher status than they would have been accorded under the system in force at the same period in the Union. Though, moreover, the most recent policy in the Union has been announced as looking forward to creating in its Bantu areas a system which will restore to the traditional Authorities a position analogous to that enjoyed in the British dependencies under the régime known as that of 'indirect rule', all the indications nevertheless point to the likelihood that they will in fact be accorded in practice a less important position than that which has hitherto been enjoyed by the Native Authorities of the High Commission Territories. It is therefore not unnatural that one should look for indications of the views now held on the subject of transfer by other sections of the African population than the traditional Native Authorities or their supporters.

The Legislative Councils established in Basutoland by the constitutional reform of 1959, and in Bechuanaland by that of 1960 may be criticized in some quarters as falling short in respect of the constitutional powers they enjoy, but these bodies will afford (as Tshekedi Khama hoped) an independent avenue of undoubted value for the expression of opinion on such cardinal issues as the incorporation of the Territories in the South African Republic. There also now exist in the Territories a number of political organizations which are critical of the authority exercised by the hereditary Chiefs. There is, for example, in Basutoland a section known as the Congress Party, which at present actually holds a majority in the National Council. It is characteristic of its outlook that it is affiliated to the Pan-African Freedom Movement (Pafmecsa). In Bechuanaland there exist a variety of such sections, for instance, the Federal Party, also affiliated to Pafmecsa, the Democratic Party (mainly representing elements in the Bamangwato tribe), and the Liberal Party, which is said to represent the Bangwaketse tribe. Swaziland has a fairly strong Progressive Party, also affiliated to Pafmecsa, with a less numerous Democratic Party, and a small body known as the

Mbandzeni National Convention. All these sections seem to claim as their primary objective the achievement of independence of the Colonial Power, and some of them (most notably the Basutoland Congress Party) have petitioned the Committee on Colonialism of the United Nations (known alternatively as the Committee of Twenty-Four) for assistance in this endeavour.[12] It is noteworthy that in February 1962, the Pan-African Freedom Movement meeting at Addis Ababa passed a resolution demanding independence for the High Commission Territories.[13] It is, however, the common experience that elsewhere (as for instance in Ghana, or East Nigeria, or in the ex-French African dependencies) the parties that have been most militant in the cause of independence are also equally anxious to deprive their traditional Native Authorities of their customary position and powers. Though in Swaziland the Progressive Party appears to have agreed to accept the Swazi Paramount Chief as a 'constitutional monarch', the general attitude of the 'Independence' parties at large remains opposed to any recognition of the position of traditional as opposed to elective Authorities. But it remains equally true that neither the new legislative bodies created by the reforms of 1959 and 1960, nor any of the 'independence' Parties just referred to, have shown any desire for incorporation in the Republic of South Africa. Nor indeed does it seem that there is any evidence of an interest shown by these parties in the recent legislation regarding the powers to be given to the projected 'Bantustans' for the creation of which the Republic is now making itself responsible.

[12] *International Bulletin of the Africa Institute*, March 1963, p. 44.
[13] Hsinhua News Agency, 10 Feb. 1962.

VI

THE PRESENT ATTITUDE IN THE REPUBLIC TO INCORPORATION

THE claim made by the Union Ministers for the transfer of the three Territories to its administration was pressed on Great Britain for over forty years from the date when it was first put forward by General Botha in 1913. The British reaction to this claim has admittedly revealed a measure of hesitancy, and at times even of evasion, which must have appeared unworthy of a great nation. But some excuse for this may be admitted when it is realized that for the British this claim acquired increasingly the character of a moral rather than a political problem. This was only dimly apprehended at first, but the problem increased in gravity with the progress of the notable change in British social life which, as the century advanced, created a new outlook on the objectives to be sought in the realm of domestic politics. The British public had become increasingly concerned with the need for the improvement of the standards of life in what had hitherto been the less considered sections of its population, and in proportion tended to take also a more liberal view of the claims for recognition made by the inhabitants of the British dependencies. It is of some significance that the grant of Responsible Government to the Transvaal and the Orange Free State in 1906 and 1907 and the enactment of the Act of Union in 1909, on which the Liberal Government of that day placed its faith in the growth of liberal policies in South Africa, coincided so nearly with the enactment of the Morley–Minto reforms of 1909 which guaranteed to the people of India a more effective share in the administrative life of their country.

It is true that the hopes for the growth of liberal policies in South Africa which were entertained during the passing of the

Act of Union failed to bear fruit, and the proof of their failure is now to be seen most decisively in the course taken by the Republic of South Africa. A recent study made of this development has emphasized that the transfer of power to the Northern Republics in 1906 and 1907 and the assent accorded to the unification of South Africa in 1909 were made in the spirit of an age when men still believed in progress and assumed the likelihood that liberties would grow and broaden. 'The concession of self-government, which had then seemed so generous, had infinite possibilities. The Union of South Africa might have become an enlightened liberal community. That it has become something so very different is a shocking setback to our liberalizing policy, a refutation of our doctrine of progress.'[1] The view thus expressed regarding the declaration of the Republic of South Africa may be felt by some to be overstated in its condemnation of the spirit in which the affairs of the Republic are being conducted. But it remains true that, in so far as the interests of the people of the three Territories are concerned, the result has justified the forebodings which lay behind the British reaction to the claim for incorporation of the Territories that had been pressed so strongly by the Ministers of the Union. That reaction did not merely represent disappointment that the Union Government had refused to consider the general extension of the Cape Native franchise, nor was it due to any doubt regarding the good faith of the Union Government when it agreed in 1939 to abide by the conditions laid down for the transfer of the Territories.[2] It has had a deeper cause. It points to the fact that the growing insistence today on the rigid application of the doctrine of segregation implies that so long as that policy holds the field, the non-European peoples of South Africa cannot aspire to any effective share in the government of the country, whatever may be the functions they may be permitted to discharge in the local control of the areas specially designated for their occupation.

---

[1] C. E. Carrington, in *International Affairs*, January 1962, p. 33. Compare *Cambridge History of the British Empire*, loc. cit., p. 346.
[2] See pp. 84–85 above.

The question must now be faced, whether the understanding of 1909 that the administration of the Territories would at some time be transferred to the Union should now be considered as retaining validity in regard to the Republic of South Africa. The Schedule to the Act of 1909 which constituted the Union carried a clear implication that if the Union agreed to abide by the conditions for transfer embodied in it, the transfer would undoubtedly take place. Though the Government of Great Britain found reason to repent of having given so clear an indication of its intention, policy forbade it to inform the Union at any time that it could no longer hope that effect would be given to this intention. It is noteworthy that when the Union was preparing to declare itself a Republic outside the Commonwealth, it took steps to legislate for the repeal of any enactments which might stand in the way of this change of its constitutional status. In 1962 it passed an Act[3] which rescinded some sixty-six enactments which fell into this category, but it specially reserved from repeal Sections 56, 115, 150, and 151 of the 1909 Act and also the Schedule attached to it. It is possible that in so doing the Union Government desired to keep alive the implications contained in the Schedule; or it may be that it desired to put on record a reminder that it had in its Memorandum of 1939[4] explicitly accepted the terms embodied in the Schedule for regulating the process of transfer of the Territories to the Union. When in May 1962 the British Government took occasion on its own part to repeal any enactments which stood in the way of this constitutional change, it passed an Act[5] repealing some twenty-nine enactments but took no steps to repeal the South Africa Act of 1909 referred to above. It was explained in the course of the debate[6] that in the view of the British Government this Act lapsed when South Africa left the Commonwealth, and it was included in a list of such Acts which were sent to the Vote Office for record. Elsewhere the expression used was 'we consider that as a

---

[3] Entitled The South Africa Act, 1962.   [4] See p. 84 above.
[5] Act 10 & 11 Eliz. 2, c. 23.
[6] *Hansard*, House of Lords, 12 April 1962, Cols. 562–642.

result of the constitutional change this Act is spent and we have so informed the South African Government'.[7] Whatever the implication to be attached to the legal expression thus used, it is clear to the layman that the operation which the Schedule of the Act of Union contemplated was the transfer of the Territories from the administration of one of the British Sovereign's Dominions to that of another. But this operation had now become impossible of performance since the second Dominion had ceased to exist. It would appear that the Government of the Republic has in fact accepted this conclusion, since Dr. Verwoerd stated in the House of Assembly that the question of incorporation of the Territories was no longer an active matter in the policy of the Republic.

This must not, however, be taken as evidence that the Republic no longer retains any interest in the acquisition of some form of control over the Territories. Their incorporation could never, it is true, have been seen as a possible asset of any great economic importance. Swaziland no doubt has mineral and agricultural resources[8] which would make it a not unimportant adjunct to the Transvaal, but Basutoland is only made a possible asset by virtue of its 'migrant' labour, and Bechuanaland, with its vast area of arid waste, would seem to be a liability rather than an asset. One must not, however, underestimate the genuine anxiety with which Union Ministers had again and again pressed for the early transfer of the Territories, whether their motive may have been to ensure uniformity in their Native policy, or to prevent a breach in the provision they proposed to make for national defence, or indeed merely to acquire for the Union the added prestige of forcing Britain to surrender to it these small units which recall a period when the Union itself was a dependent unit of the British Empire. There has now been added what appears to be an even more pertinent reason for the acquisition of control over the Territories. This has had its origin in the measure to which the Nationalist Party has accustomed itself to look to the expansion of the criminal law as a bulwark for defence of its

[7] Ibid., Col. 575.   [8] *Annual Report, Swaziland, 1961.*

political philosophy. It resents in consequence the refuge which the Territories may afford to citizens of the Republic who seek to avoid the penalties provided by law for those who urge the reform of the system approved by the party in power.

Incidents due to this cause have lately received much attention in both the South African and the London Press. In 1961 public opinion in Basutoland was shown to be seriously concerned when a minor political figure in Pondoland, who had escaped from detention under the Emergency Regulations of the Union, and had taken refuge in Basuto country, was there seized by a party of South African police and taken back to the Union. He was eventually released from custody in January 1962, as the result of proceedings taken at the instance of the High Commissioner in a superior Court of the Republic.[9] In 1962 it was reported in the Press that public opinion in the Republic was reacting strongly to suggestions coming from the South African Security Police that use was being made of Bechuanaland as an 'escape route' by agitators who came under the scope of the Acts ostensibly directed against Communism, though these were in fact utilized mainly for suppressing any opinion unfavourable to the Government of the Republic. A demand was being made in the Nationalist Press that the High Commissioner should put pressure on the Territory to control this cause of annoyance to the Republic.[10] In December 1962 notices were served by the Pretoria Courts on all persons who belonged to the Swaziland Progressive Party, the Basutoland Congress Party, and the Bechuanaland People's Party.[11] Though such notices could have effect only if members of these parties visited the Republic, the procedure adopted seemed to suggest that a prosecution could rely on evidence from agents of the Republic in the Territories concerned. In April 1963 allegations were published that a leader of the South African Pan-Africanist Congress had been 'kidnapped' by South

[9] See *Hansard*, House of Lords, 1 May 1962, Col. 1014.
[10] *The Times*, 16 November 1962.
[11] Ibid., 29 December 1962.

African police in Basutoland.[12] There is some doubt as to the
truth of this, but it seems true that the Basutoland Administration had found it necessary to refuse a demand from the
Republic that it should take action to prosecute this person for
making speeches which were described as 'inflammatory'. It
was not unnatural that Basutoland should permit police from
the Republic to collaborate in searching for members of
Poqo, since this was widely regarded as a criminal organization, but it is ominous that the Nationalist Press of
South Africa, which some years ago had characterized Basutoland as 'the home of Communism',[13] could now add that the
police of the Republic considered the Territory to be the 'nerve
centre' of the Poqo organization. Early in April the Pretoria
Courts sentenced thirty-seven Africans who had left the Republic without valid travel documents. They had been arrested
by the police in Northern Rhodesia and returned to the
Republic via Bechuanaland.[14]

It is readily understandable that the growing tension created
by incidents such as these must have caused much disquiet to
the British Government, and it is no doubt to this that we
must look for the explanation of an order passed on 5 June
1963, which declared Mr. Patrick Duncan to be a 'prohibited
entrant' to any of the three Territories.[15] He had formerly
been a member of the Administrative Services in Basutoland,
and after retirement he became conspicuous as the editor of
the Liberal 'pro-African' journal *Contact* in Cape Town. He
was on a visit to England when the notice was published, but
had for some time taken refuge in Basutoland because of an
order issued by the Government of the Republic restricting
his movements. It was incidentally *Contact* that had a
short time before claimed that their independence had made
the Territories 'an oasis of freedom in a world of *apartheid.*'

In this instance the desire to avoid an open breach with the
Republic appears to have influenced the decision taken by

[12] Ibid., 6 April 1963. [13] See p. 93 above. [14] *The Times*, 5 April 1963.
[15] Ibid., 5 June 1963. On 12 June Mr. M. Harmel, a South African
journalist, was excluded from entry to Bechuanaland (ibid., 13 June 1963).

the British Government. But apart from this the Republic is clearly in a position to exercise direct pressure on the Territories themselves, and it can do so by measures which will be entirely within its own competence. There would, for instance, be a severe loss to the revenue of the Territories if the Government of the Republic were now to insist on recalculating in accordance with present realities the amount of customs and excise duties received by them as the result of the Agreements made in 1903 and 1910.[16] In Bechuanaland these receipts amount to about 30 per cent. of the total income (excluding receipts from British Treasury grants or grants under the Colonial Development and Welfare Acts). In Basutoland they amount to about 15 per cent.[17] There would be a loss of a type which might be felt more directly by the African people of the Territories if the Republic were now to exercise its right to modify the system of local quotas which regulate the export of produce from a Territory, or by changes of a similar nature in the regulations for the import of livestock, or by restrictions on the employment of 'migrant' labour. Some of these measures might certainly bring some disadvantage to the Republic itself, but it might well be willing to face this contingency.

The impact on the Territories of measures of this nature taken by the Republic would no doubt vary in its intensity. Speaking in general terms, Swaziland would probably be least affected. It is already more self-sufficient in its own economy than are the other two Territories. The prosperous Havelock Mine (now one of the five main producers of asbestos in the world) and the industries created by the extensive forest plantations (covering at present some 169,000 acres) provide employment for what seems likely to become a stable labour force; and there will be a further demand for local labour when the iron ore deposits on the Bonvu Ridge are developed. The iron ore will be delivered under contract to two Japanese concessionaire companies, after transport to Lourenço Marques by a new railway line already begun and

[16] See p. 41 above.   [17] *The Times*, 27 April 1961.

due to be completed in 1964.[18] Bechuanaland is to some small
degree independent of the Republic, in so far as some part of
its local production of livestock has access by rail to an alternative market in Southern Rhodesia and the Congo. But the
value of this is greatly reduced by the long haul involved, nor
is it likely that Rhodesia will develop any considerable demand
for surplus Bechuana labour. As for Basutoland, it is difficult
to see what new resource the Territory could find if the
Republic adopted any measure which would restrict the
market for its export of wool or the demand for its labour in
the Transvaal mines. There seemed at one time a possibility
that its position might give it a certain measure of bargaining
power if the extensive project of hydro-electric development
from the Orange River and its affluents proved to require the
use by the Republic of the lower slopes of the Drakensberg
Mountains.[19] But it has now been stated that none of the great
dams designed to serve the irrigation or the hydro-electric
objectives of this project will be sited in the Territory.[20]

It is clear, therefore, that the Territories would be vulnerable
in varying degrees to measures which the Republic might take
in matters affecting their economic life. Dr. Verwoerd had
already warned them in 1961 of the possibility that such
measures might be taken. Thus in September 1962, speaking
at the Orange Free State Nationalist Party Congress, he said
that in a few months negotiations would take place to decide
the future relationship between the Republic and the High
Commission Territories. Their people, he said, had hitherto
been accorded the same privileges as Africans from South
Africa's own African areas, since until recently it was assumed
that they would one day become part of South Africa's Bantu
areas. But during the premiership of Dr. Malan, he added,
Great Britain had started developments in the Territories
towards their independence. 'The relationship with them has

18 *The Times*, 15 and 20 September 1961.
19 *Optima*, March 1963, p. 32 and *Johannesburg Star*, 11 January 1962.
20 Department of Information, South African Embassy in London, Press
Notice, April 1962. For the project of irrigation generally see 'Morse
Report', referred to on p. 48 above, and also *Optima*, March 1963, p. 30.

now to be placed on the basis of relationship with foreign States.' Speaking on 1 October in the Transvaal, he said that Basutoland and other countries being given their independence by Great Britain 'could well become a danger to South Africa, for a weak neighbour could become a danger if good relations were not maintained.'

It may be accordingly of some advantage to explain here the situation in regard to the entry of 'migrant labour' from the Territories as it stood in May 1962. Under the South African Immigrant Regulation Act of 1913 all persons, whatever their nationality or race, might be required to produce a passport or an approved travel document; aliens required a special permit to reside in the Republic and were also required to report their movements to the South African police (Aliens Registration Act 36 of 1939 and Aliens Act of 1937). Africans from the High Commission Territories required an approved travel document to enter South Africa or to travel through it in transit. These documents also enabled them to enter any 'unrestricted' areas in order to take up employment already arranged on farms or in industry or to seek work. It was, however, the policy of the Government not to allow women from the Territories to enter even 'unrestricted' areas. To enter urban or proclaimed areas, Africans from the Territories required a special permit under the Natives (Urban Areas) Act of 1945; if they had no such permit, they might be prosecuted or deported to their homes. Africans in 'proclaimed' areas might seek work only under the Labour Bureaux permits, which are not granted to Africans from the Territories. All Africans of these Territories were for the present to be allowed to remain on farms in 'unrestricted' areas; but if they became unemployed they were required to return to their homes. It would seem, however, that the laws regulating the possession of passports were not in practice rigorously enforced by the Union authorities where Africans from the Territories were concerned; it was, however, stated in April 1963 that the law relating to the possession of passports would in future be applied to persons entering the Republic from the Territories or entering the Territories from the Republic.[21] It is too early to say yet how far this regulation will now be applied in practice, or to what extent the movement of labour will be consequently affected.

It will be obvious that the existing legislation gives extensive power to the Government of the Republic to interfere by regulation with the movement of labour from the Territories, should it so desire. But though Africans in the Territories have been warned of this position, the Republic has not so far shown any explicit intention to use these powers for bringing pressure on the Territories in order to influence their incorporation in the Republic, though it has of course on occasion used sections of the law in the interest of the maintenance of 'public safety' or for control of the political movements directed against its own policy.[22] It may on the other hand reasonably be held that the Republic may prefer to delay any attempt to acquire control by exerting pressure on the Territories, while awaiting the result of inducements held out to them of accepting the status of the 'Bantu Homelands' or 'Bantustans' now in process of establishment under its aegis. It will be remembered that in 1955 the Press organ of the Nationalist Party in the Union suggested that Great Britain should be moved to develop the Territories as Native Reserves, thus qualifying them for partaking in the special status forecast for these Reserves by the recent Tomlinson Commission Report.[23] The proposal made in that Report actually dates further back to suggestions made by Dr. W. W. M. Eiselen, whose Commission on Native Education in the Union began its deliberations in 1950.[24] In 1950 the British quarterly journal *The Round Table* suggested that a time might come when a position as a 'Bantustan', as it was then envisaged by Dr. Eiselen, might have an attraction for the High Commission Territories. This conception, as the article went on to say,

envisages a vertical instead of a horizontal division of the Union into two separate and self-contained communities, each equipped with

[21] *The Times*, 3 April 1963.   [22] See p. 108 above.   [23] See p. 94 above.
[24] *Commission on Native Education, 1949–50* (U.G. No. 55, 1951), and see *African Survey*, p. 1149.

its own political institutions and developing on its own lines . . . a Bantustan would [thus] become a separate political and economic entity, possessing at least self-government and not subject to direct European control.[25]

The considered policy of the Republic in respect of the creation of units of this character was formally stated by Dr. Verwoerd in a speech delivered in the House of Assembly on 23 January 1962. He then announced the intention of his Government to avail itself of the terms of the Bantu Self-Government Act in order to create the first 'Bantustan' in the area occupied by the Xhosa-speaking peoples of the Transkei.[26] There is some reason to hold that the term 'Bantustan' is not that now favoured by the Nationalist Party, and there may be some change in this respect, but meanwhile it may not be inappropriate to discuss whether the terms designed for the Xhosa-speaking people of the Transkei are in fact such as are likely to persuade the inhabitants of the three Territories to seek the sanction of Great Britain to join the ranks of the 'Bantustans'.

[25] *The Round Table*, March 1950, p. 214.
[26] *Rand Daily Mail*, 24 January 1962; *Cape Times*, 31 March 1962; *African Affairs* (Journal of Royal African Society), April 1962, pp. 97–103.

VII

THE TERRITORIES AND THE PROJECTED 'BANTUSTANS'

THE scheme of legislation announced by Dr. Verwoerd in January 1962 was embodied in proposals which were sent for consideration to the Transkeian Territorial Authority. They were referred by it to a 'Recess Committee' of twenty-seven Council Members appointed by it for this purpose. On 4 May 1962 the Recess Committee reported that it had considered and approved the scheme, which it described as being one 'for the self-government of the territory'.[1] Some difference of opinion had, as it said, occurred regarding the composition of the Legislature to be created. There had been those who favoured the reduction of the number of traditional or appointed Chiefs and a proportional increase in the number of elected members, but the majority of the Committee had preferred the composition proposed in the scheme as drafted by the Government.[2] The Transkei Constitution Bill, embodying the proposals, was placed before Parliament in January 1963 and adopted with only minor modifications in May. The Nationalist Party Press claimed that it afforded proof that 'the positive side of apartheid' was now well on its way; 'the principle of separate development would no longer be a myth but a practical fact'.[3]

The scheme embodies a number of principles of much significance when viewed from the standpoint of the residents of the High Commission Territories. First, it makes clear that in this, as in any subsequent proposals for the recognition of

[1] *Report of Recess Committee of the Transkeian Territorial Authority* (9 May 1962); *International Bulletin of the Africa Institute*, Pretoria, No. 2 (March 1963).
[2] See, on this point, *The Round Table*, March 1963, p. 206.
[3] *Sunday Times*, 10 March 1963.

Bantu units of local self-government, primary importance will be attached to the preservation or reproduction of the traditional institutions of the Bantu, such as the tribal Chieftainship. It was stated in the Cape Town Press that Dr. Verwoerd had himself been in favour of a majority of elected members in the Transkei, but that he subsequently waived this opinion in view of the strength of the emphasis laid by the Recess Committee on the proposal for a majority of traditional or appointed Chiefs.[4] In the second place, representation in the local legislature will be confined to Bantu citizens; the Committee categorically rejected 'any conception of a multi-racial parliament'. Thirdly, the field of powers to be exercised by the local Administration would exclude defence, foreign relations, railways, immigration, and any question regarding the constitution of the Transkeian Authority. It is noticeable that the Recess Committee left over for further discussion the question whether there should be any change in the system of administration of justice, as for example by the institution of a Transkeian High Court, having the status of a Provincial Divisional Court in the Republic. Fourthly, citizenship qualifying for the vote was defined as shared by the Bantu people domiciled in the Transkei, Xhosa-speaking people elsewhere in the Republic of South Africa, and Sotho-speaking Bantu related by descent to the Sotho-speaking tribes in the Transkei. Fifthly, the Cabinet of five to eight Ministers, with the Prime Minister at their head, when once elected, could not be removed without the permission of the President of the Republic, who would also have the power of either assenting to legislation, or of remitting it to the Transkeian Legislative Assembly for further consideration.[5] In many respects, therefore, the authority reserved to the Government of the Republic would resemble that now exercised by the High Commissioner in respect of the three Territories.

---

[4] *The Times*, 15 December 1962, and *International Bulletin of the Africa Institute*, Pretoria, No. 2 (March, 1963), p. 39; *The Round Table*, March 1963, p. 30.

[5] *Report of Recess Committee*, paras. 28 and 30.

The immediate result of the publication of these proposals for the new 'Bantustan' was to cause very serious apprehension among the White residents in the Transkei. These have been stated in the Press as numbering 16,000 in all, as against 1,300,000 Bantu, but they have been credited with possession of a stake in the area valued at £6,500,000.[6] Moreover there occurred early in February 1963 an outrage in the Transkei area resulting in the murder of three White adults and two children, and though it is not certain that the incident had a racial origin, the feeling in the White population was such as to cause a widespread demand that the Government of the Republic should take special measures for its protection. These apprehensions were increased by newspaper reports that gangs of 'Poqo', a terrorist organization, had invaded the Transkei.[7]

Apart, however, from the immediate trouble created by the fears of the White population in the Transkei, there are problems of a more general character which the Republic may have to meet when it seeks to extend the number of the Bantustans. For the Transkei presented an exceptional case, in so far as it had a long experience in the exercise of the procedure of local self-government, and had a relatively homogeneous area in respect of the tribal distribution of its population. With the passing of the Glen Grey Act of 1894, parts of the Transkei had been chosen for an experiment in a system of local government by Native Councils, and a number of such Councils were gradually amalgamated until the United Transkeian General Council (the 'Bunga') took final form in 1931 and became recognized as the most effective African organ of local government in the Union.[8] This position was not materially affected by the passing of the Bantu Authorities Act of 1951, which gave expression to the principles of Nationalist policy relating to the Bantu section of the population; the only change was that the 'Territorial Authority of the Transkei' took over the functions which had been discharged

[6] *The Times*, 2 March 1963.   [7] Ibid., 5 April 1963.
[8] *An African Survey*, pp. 421–2, 426–7.

by the Transkeian United Council. Historical developments had thus combined with physical and social factors to indicate the Transkei as the most appropriate area for the creation of the first Bantustan. It will not be equally simple to designate its successors. Zululand seems indicated as the most homogeneous area available as a second choice, but there events have already created serious doubts whether the Zulu Chiefs will welcome a development similar to that of the Transkei. In the Ciskei (the Kaffraria so well known in South African history) a system of local Councils was established in 1920, and in 1934 these were federated in the Ciskeian General Council. But since in this case each local Council has remained in charge of its own revenue and expenditure, the Ciskeian General Council has never occupied the same position as the Transkeian United Council. The area is also much less homogeneous in tribal constitution, and it is to that extent less adapted for development as a Bantustan. Farther afield, in the widely scattered Native Reserves of the Republic, the problem will be even more difficult. The Native Reserves comprise in all 260 separate areas, which vary from that of the Transkei (58 million acres) to that of the Premier Mine Reserve, with only 40,000 acres. Their greatly deteriorated lands will, it has been calculated, require the expenditure of £104,000,000 and take at least ten years before they can show signs of improvement.[9]

Apart from the difficulty of finding an area as suitable as the Transkei for future Bantustans there may well be a serious obstacle in regard to the provision of finance. No real measure of self-rule can be claimed for any government, however free it may be in theory from outside control, if it does not in fact possess a reasonable measure of viability in the matter of its own finance. The Transkei has an annual budget of about £6,100,000, but the revenue derived from purely local sources appears to be only about £1,700,000.[10] Its administration cannot without outside aid engage on any serious measure

[9] L. Marquard, *South Africa's Internal Boundaries* (1958), p. 12.
[10] *The Times*, 29 March 1963.

of social or economic development. It will be even more difficult for successive Bantustans to achieve any measure of autonomy unless their constitution provides them from the first with domestic sources of revenue which will give them a reasonable measure of viability.

No one can deny that there are certain aspects of administration in which the Union, or the Republic in its turn, has shown readiness to incur a liberal measure of expenditure in African interests. They claim to have spent in the last decade over £100,000,000 in the housing of Bantu families in the urban areas. They also claim a higher proportion of expenditure on health measures and on education than any of the African territories under British control. Already four out of five Bantu children in the Republic are at school, and every year now sees an addition of 2,000 to the existing total of 27,000 Bantu teachers.[11] There were in 1961 as many as 4,500 Bantu School Committees. These, however, are figures which relate to the Republic as a whole, including the very large Bantu population in the urban areas, the mines, and the European farms, as well as those living in the Native Reserves. What, it may be asked, is likely to be done in order to prove that Nationalist policy contemplates a real régime of self-rule for the Bantu areas which are now to be recognized as separated by the doctrine of *apartheid* from contact with the White population? Consideration of this aspect of their separate life has not been entirely neglected. A sum of £12 million was earmarked for expenditure during 1963 in the 'Homelands of the Bantu'. A Five-Year Planning and Development Corporation was to be appointed in 1963 to examine schemes of economic assistance to the Xhosa areas of the Transkei. But how far these measures will lead to the creation of any recognizable measure of financial viability in the Bantustans is at present difficult to estimate.

The Bantustans, geographically scattered and unco-ordinated, must apparently continue to occupy the markedly

[11] Dr. H. Muller, 'Separate Development in South Africa', *African Affairs*, January 1963, p. 61.

inferior position in point of industrial development which is now their lot, and this is not likely to be greatly improved by the creation of that 'fringe of border industries' which forms so highly speculative an element in the Tomlinson Commission's scheme. The improvement in the agricultural production of the 'Bantustans' which would, the Commission hoped, follow from the adoption of the system of individual as opposed to collective land tenure, has been frustrated by the decision of the Government in favour of retaining the 'traditional procedure of the Bantu'. The policy adopted in this latter field has been claimed by the Nationalist Party as a generous concession to Bantu feeling, but there is another side which has been adversely criticized by leaders of African opinion. To them such so-called concessions fall into the same category as the educational system now being devised for the Bantu,[12] which differs widely from that being provided for Europeans, and is subject to such limitations as to be viewed by advanced African opinion as likely to retard rather than to promote progress towards the attainment of that part in the future régime of the Republic to which it has begun to aspire. It is possible that this consideration may weigh with the intellectuals who comprise the 'Independence' Parties in the Territories rather than with their African population at large. But whether or not this proves to be the case, it is highly probable that a large section of Africans in the Territories will react strongly against acceptance of the political status of a Bantustan, since this will close to them the possibility of attaining that measure of autonomy which will qualify the Territory for inclusion among the units of the United Nations. It is inclusion among these units which is the final test accepted by them (like other Colonial peoples) as signalizing the achievement of full nationhood.

Since one of the objects of the present study is to examine how far the 'Bantustans' will present such features as seem likely to induce all or any of the Territories to join their

[12] Ruth Sloan Associates (Helen Kitchen, Ed.), *The Educated African* (New York, Heinemann, 1962), p. 268 ff.

number, it may be well to note shortly the position which the Territories themselves now present in these matters of finance and political advancement. There is no question that there was a past period when the British Government showed small interest in their economic or social development. During the discussions at the National Convention which preceded the passing of the Union Act of 1909,[13] some delegates referred to the 'niggardly' attitude observed by Great Britain in regard to the financing of development in the three Territories. In 1933 Dr. Malan also found occasion to charge Great Britain with neglecting the Protectorates in this respect. The criticism voiced in 1909 was in great measure justified by the earlier experience of the Territories. A Treasury grant might at that time be made to one or another of them in order to prevent a budget deficit, but the British Treasury exercised rigorous control in order to ensure that the annual expenditure should be limited to the bare necessities of the local Administrations. It is clear, however, that something of a new era in the grant of assistance specifically designed for purposes of development commenced as the result of Mr. L. Amery's visit to the Territories in 1927, followed by the publication of the Financial Reports of Sir Alan Pim in 1932 and the following years.[14] The scale of assistance thus given was substantially increased by the more generous grants made under the Colonial Development and Welfare Act passed in 1940 and extended in 1955. The Territories have of recent years also received the benefit of the expenditure incurred by the Colonial Development Corporation, which was established in order to give effect to the provisions of the Overseas Resources Development Acts 1948–59. There are in the Territories a number of economic projects which the Corporation has originated or in which it has agreed to participate.

Some indication of the assistance afforded to the Territories by the contributions made by Great Britain under these various heads may be gathered from the following figures. The United Kingdom Treasury grants made during the years 1956

[13] See p. 27 ff above.   [14] See p. 70 above.

to 1963 have amounted in all to £9,132,236. The grants made under the Colonial Development and Welfare Acts in the years 1940 to 1963 have amounted to a total of £11,674,569, and Great Britain is providing a sum of £3,477,712 for Treasury assistance up to the end of 1964. The Colonial Development Corporation has since 1949 committed itself to a total expenditure in the Territories amounting to £21,317,000 of which £16,223,000 had been expended up to the end of 1962. Of this last expenditure Swaziland has been the major recipient, and it has been reported in the Press that in the last twenty years a sum of about £40 million has also been contributed to development in Swaziland by private capital engaged in industrial or similar enterprise.[15]

During the discussions in the National Convention of 1908 there were also suggestions that the British Government had up to that time done little for the political development of the Territories. That criticism also was not without some justification, so far as regards the period preceding the passing of the Act of Union. The system of 'parallel rule' which left so wide a field of local control to the traditional Native Authorities undoubtedly succeeded in the first instance in securing a peaceful settlement of the Territories and a general acceptance of British control, though such results as it achieved in social or political advancement inevitably varied with the character of the Native Authorities themselves. But the reforms effected by the Bechuanaland Proclamations of 1934 and 1943, those of 1948 in Basutoland, and those of 1944 and 1950 in Swaziland,[16] though primarily directed to regularizing the position of the Native Authorities in relation to the official Administrations, had important reactions also in organizing the means for the expression of public opinion.

Subsequent constitutional changes gave to Basutoland in 1960 a constitution of which the chief feature was the introduction of forty elected members into the National Council and three elected members into the Executive Council, who thus

[15] *Optima*, March 1962, p. 17.
[16] *Native Administration*, Pt. V, pp. 81–85, 224–8, and 388–93.

have a position corresponding to that of Ministers. After the constitution had been operating for less than eighteen months a Commission was appointed as the result of a Resolution of the National Council which advocated a constitution more nearly approaching that of Responsible Government. It had by the end of 1962 heard evidence from 640 persons and received 1,200 memoranda. In Bechuanaland there is now a Legislative Council of thirty-five members, of whom twenty-one are elected; the ten Africans are elected by the African Council, many of whom are themselves elected.[17] In Swaziland there existed until recent years a system which originated about 1890, under which there were in effect two parallel systems of government, one for Europeans and one for the control of African affairs. Thus there was a European Advisory Council, and a Swazi National Council which in theory consisted of heads of households, but in practice was attended only by Chiefs and a number of senior commoners. Prolonged discussions have now reached agreement that it is time for a revision of these arrangements. It seems, however, that there has been a disagreement between the scheme put forward by the Colonial Office, which provided for a preponderance of African voters, and a scheme advocated by a large number of Swazi representatives of more conservative views. Their scheme pointed to a constitution in which the Paramount Chief would be recognized as 'constitutional monarch' of a 'protected state', and it would provide a Legislature consisting of a fixed proportion of Europeans and Africans, both chosen by popular vote.

It was apparently the measures taken in the three Territories in 1960 and the following year which constituted that 'development towards independence' which Dr. Verwoerd, speaking in the Orange Free State Nationalist Congress in September 1962, seems to have regarded as constituting a warning light.[18] They may in truth prove to point further forward in the

[17] Speech to U.N. Assembly by Sir Patrick Dean, 26 November 1962, printed at p. 99 ff. of *African Affairs*, No. 247, April 1963.
[18] See p. 111 above.

direction of political advance than the measure of self-government now to be accorded to the Xhosa people of the Transkei.
It may, for instance, be true that the section of the Basuto
National Council which has recently taken the lead in pressing
for a constitution of Responsible Government consists of what
an American author has recently described as a body of
'militant, radical Pan-Africanists',[19] but the fact remains that
the National Council by a majority vote has shown itself
genuinely interested in securing a very much larger proportion
of members selected by a widely popular vote.

But before ending this examination of the points in the
projected Bantustans which are calculated to attract the
approval or the disapproval of the people of the three Territories, there remains one other aspect of the Bantustan scheme
which cannot be overlooked. Dr. Verwoerd's reference to it
seemed to assume that the scheme would remain as a standing
feature in the constitution of the Republic. But is there in
truth any solid ground for this assumption? The projected
system of Bantustans may be said to have had its origin in the
answer given by the Tomlinson Commission to the main
problem which had been set before it by the Government of
the Union. It was in effect commissioned to inquire whether
there existed any practicable alternative to the eventual recognition of an element of multi-racialism in the constitution of
the Union, a question of critical importance, since the
Nationalist Party was convinced that any measure which
allowed this principle to find a place in the constitution would
sound the death knell of European civilization in South Africa.
The Commission found the answer in what has been not
inaptly described as the creation of a 'White-dominated state,
with Black satellites orbiting around it'.[20] But there are obvious
difficulties in accepting such a solution as practicable over any
prolonged period of time. It was based on assumptions
regarding the relative growth of the White and Black populations during the next forty years which are in the highest
degree speculative. It contemplated that there would continue

[19] Sloan and Kitchen, op. cit., p. 281. [20] *Optima*, March 1963, p. 22.

to exist within the White area a very large African population. It has been estimated that in 1951 there were 2·6 million Africans on the European farms and 2·3 million in European urban areas.[21] The number who are likely to remain in the future is a matter of conjecture, but it is certain to be very considerable. It will, moreover, represent a new type of modernized African which has become part of the Republic in recent years. The Government of the Republic has in a recent publication described this population as possessing higher standards of intelligence and social life than Africans in any other country south of the Sahara.[22] It is now, and will as time goes on become increasingly essential to the maintenance of the industries on which the modern prosperity of the White population of the Republic is being built up. Its members will become the more inclined to invade the political field of the White community because many of them will have experience of exercising a vote in the affairs of one or other of the proposed Bantustans. It will consequently represent an element of unsettlement which may make it difficult to maintain the political régime of the Republic in the form sought by the Nationalist Party.

On a broad view, therefore, it would seem that the scheme of Satellite States is unlikely to become as wide in scope or to prove as durable as has been anticipated by the Nationalist Party. In any case, on that and the other grounds described above, it is not likely that it will secure the adhesion of the three Territories.

[21] Marquard, op. cit., p. 3.
[22] *The Progress of the Bantu People towards Nationhood* (Pretoria, 1962).

VIII
CONCLUSIONS

IF, as seems likely, the three Territories do not agree to be incorporated into the Republic of South Africa, we may assume that Great Britain will retain her control over them, though we may also assume that, following the fashion of the time, there will be a tendency to relax control wherever it may seem politic or prudent to do so. There is no recognized standard which a controlling Power can apply in judging whether a dependent territory is fit for the grant of full independence, and the answer to the problem often tends in effect to be a pragmatic reaction to pressures arising from within the dependency or from outside it in the form of what arrogates to itself the claim to express world opinion. But whatever may be the arguments which may bring a metropolitan Power to the threshold of a decision on this point, common prudence dictates the wisdom of considering whether the dependency seems able to pass the test of viability as viewed in economic and political terms. This is a test which the High Commission Territories would seem to vary in their ability to pass.

Swaziland has (as has already been pointed out) a more stable internal economy of its own than either of the two others. But the 1963 constitution (Cmnd. 2052) has revealed the same conflict between Europeans and Africans, and between traditional and progressive elements, as elsewhere in Africa. Bechuanaland on present showing stands in a different position. Though recent events (and particularly the personality of some of its chiefly families) have given much publicity to the Bamangwato tribe, the Protectorate actually contains eight separate Tribal Reserves, and though the Ngwato Reserve is in point of area and population larger than that of any other, it does not in the Native tradition rank as the 'senior' tribe; not only this, but the Ngwato tribe itself constitutes only about one-fourth of the total population of the Ngwato Reserve. Feeling between the tribes runs strongly, and there is a well-established tradition by which issues arising within the tribe, whether economic or judicial, are decided by the Ruling Chief presiding over the meeting of the tribal 'kgotla', to which all residents of the Reserve have access, and which possesses a real measure of vitality and authority.[1] It will accordingly require a considerable measure of readjustment to create out of the existing Legislature of the Territory a body complying with the standards necessary to any form of Responsible government. Not only is there this obstacle to achieving viability in the constitutional sense, but the Bechuana Protectorate, with its extensive area of approximately 223,000 square miles of relatively arid pasture, is in a financial sense the most unfavourably situated of the three Territories, and is entirely dependent on outside financial aid for executing any considerable measure of development. The possibility of the discovery of mineral resources, of which a survey is now being undertaken after a delay of many years due to conflicting tribal claims, is still very doubtful. Basutoland retains some of that tradition of tribal unity which was given to it by Moshesh, and its National Council seems to be well recognized as a body representing the interests of the Basuto people. The Council has the additional advantage that it can be regarded as entirely Bantu, the White inhabitants of the Territory being a minority so small as to be practically negligible.[2] The Territory might therefore be regarded as having a reasonable prospect of viability, save only for the obvious weakness of its financial structure.

But whatever view we may take of the capacity for self-rule acquired by the Territories, then if they remain unwilling to join the ranks of the Satellites of the Republic, they must continue under the control of Great Britain. They will not,

---

Native Administration, Pt. V, p. 287.
[2] See p. 98 above. The figure usually given (2,000 Europeans out of a total of 800,000 inhabitants) includes very many who are only short-term residents.

however, be free from the apprehension of pressure in one form
or another from their powerful neighbour, whether that proves
to be exerted in pursuit of the long-cherished desire to control
their administration, or from the resolve to prevent their forming centres of agitation by supporters of African aspirations.
Their only shield will lie in the fact that Great Britain will
retain a position which gives them in international law the
status of Protected States. We may leave out of account any
protection they may hope to secure by adherence to the new
Organization for African Unity (O.A.U.) as recently envisaged
at the Conference of Addis Ababa.[3] They could in truth
expect little from an entity whose only support lies in what a
recent French author has described as the 'mystique of
négritude'. Nor could they rest assured that the intervention
of the United Nations, in accordance with General Assembly
Resolution 1817 (XVII),[4] would protect them from the
dangers to which they are exposed. The Republic, which has
outfaced that body on the issue of South West Africa, is not
likely to be deterred by mere protestations.

In maintaining ultimate control over the Territories Great
Britain might complain that she will shoulder a liability which
will bring no corresponding advantages to her. But it is a
position which she could not avoid without a grievous loss of
self-respect. And as for the Territories, it would be well for
them to realize that liberties once lost are not easily regained
by the small peoples of the world. What would it profit the
small peoples of the Territories if they now loose their hold on
the solid fact of liberty under British rule, in order that they
may grasp at the fantasy of Independence?

[3] *The Times*, 5 May 1963; for a detailed account of the Conference see
International Bulletin of the Africa Institute, Pretoria (July 1963).
[4] Passed on 18 December 1962, this Resolution invited the United
Kingdom to suspend the present constitutions of the Territories, to hold
elections based on universal suffrage, and to take steps to return to the
inhabitants all the land taken from them.

INDEX